Jenkinson shows us what Jefferson knew two hundred years ago: we are a better people than our dehumanizing popular culture might suggest. In so doing, Jenkinson rediscovers the vital and robust Jefferson and restores our trust in boldness, optimism and self-reliance.

Landon Y. Jones, author of *William Clark and the Shaping of the West* **and former editor of "People" Magazine**

No living American understands Thomas Jefferson better than Clay Jenkinson, and his call for renewed Jeffersonian vigilance and engagement moves even this cold-hearted Hamiltonian. Thomas Jefferson was the poet and dreamer of the American founding, and his words are a constant reminder that America is more than Wall Street or the Pentagon or Silicon Valley—america thrives only when its citizens take Jefferson's words to heart and act accordingly. Clay Jenkinson offers a moving reminder to his fellow citizens of their duty to nurture the Spirit of 1776.

Stephen Knott, associate professor and research fellow, Miller Center of Public Affairs, University of Virginia

Clay Jenkinson does what no previous Jefferson scholar has been able to do—he brings Jefferson alive. Jenkinson writes passionately and elegantly about what it means to be a Jeffersonian then and now. He brings the Third President to the present, and allows us to see what parts of Jefferson's vision and message ring true today as they echo back across the centuries.

Professor Hal Bidlack, Ph.D.

Regardless of your political leanings, Jenkinson's arguments for the modern Jeffersonian's view of the world today strike home page after page. And no one chooses words or combines them so powerfully as this master of the English language.

Cindy Lewis, Helena Education Foundation

In 1925 Franklin Delano Roosevelt wrote a letter in which he said, "Jefferson brought the government back to the average voter, through insistence on fundamental principles and the education of the average voter. We need a similar campaign of education today, and perhaps we shall find another Jefferson." FDR would warmly support the work of Clay Jenkinson's book, *Becoming Jefferson's People*.

Richard Marold, chautauquan and FDR scholar

Thomas Jefferson personifies the ideals of the American dream—life, liberty and the pursuit of happiness. These ideals are the forefront of the American heart and mind but we need constant reminders to re-etch these ideals into our everyday lives. Clay Jenkinson personifies Jefferson's idealogy with painstaking academic accuracy all the while evoking his great intangible passion into the 21st century by continuing the etching process so that each reader may strive for such ideals and become Jefferson's people.

Gerald Wolfe, Attorney at Law

Becoming Jefferson's People is a clarion call for those who wish to take back their country and restore the promise offered by the American Revolution. Clay Jenkinson's powerful and provocative book not only informs the readers about the beliefs of Thomas Jefferson—which in itself is a useful service—but it just might convince readers that most Americans are in fact Jeffersonians. Those who wish enlightenment leadership, energy independence, a regulated economy, a better educated citizenry, and a government that is more responsive to the will of the people will discover that they desire what Jefferson would want were he here today. In fact, Jefferson is here today through his words, and this important book soars on its message that those words can lead to an imperative national renewal.

John Ferling, author of *Adams vs Jefferson* and *A Leap in the Dark*

Becoming Jefferson's People

If you would like an autographed book plate by this author, please send a self-addressed, first class stamped envelope to:

Marmarth Press
6015 S. Virginia St.
Ste. E, # 458
Reno, NV 89502
Attention: CSJ Autograph

ALSO BY CLAY S. JENKINSON

Published by Marmarth Press,
a division of Empire for Liberty, LLC

*The Character of Meriwether Lewis:
'Completely Metamorphosed' in the American West*

*Message on the Wind:
A Spiritual Odyssey on the Northern Plains*

Thomas Jefferson: The Man of Light

Published by Henry Holt and Company, LLC

*The Lewis and Clark Companion
An Encyclopedic Guide to the Voyage of Discovery*

Published by
The North Dakota Humanities Council, Inc.

*A Lewis & Clark Chapbook:
Lewis & Clark in North Dakota*

Published by Humanities Iowa and
Iowa Lewis & Clark Bicentennial Commission

Lewis & Clark in Iowa

Published by the
State Historical Society of North Dakota

*A Vast and Open Plain:The Writings of the Lewis and Clark
Expedition in North Dakota, 1804 – 1806*
Edited and with an introduction by Clay S. Jenkinson

Becoming Jefferson's People:
Re-inventing the American Republic in the Twenty-first Century

Clay S. Jenkinson

Marmarth Press
Nevada

Published by Marmarth Press
An imprint of Empire for Liberty, LLC.
6015 S. Virginia St. Ste. E, # 458
Reno, Nevada 89502
1.800.274.1240
1.775.828.5384

This book is printed on acid-free paper

ISBN 1-930806-22-1

10 9 8 7 6 5 4 3 2

Front cover artwork credits:
Edgehill Jefferson
Jefferson, Thomas, 1743-1826
Oil on canvas, 1805
National Portrait Gallery, Smithsonian Institute, and Mon-
ticello, Thomas Jefferson Memorial Foundation; Gift of the
Regents of the Smithsonian Institution, and the Enid and
Crosby Kemper Foundation

Design by Erin McGee

Library of Congress Control Number: 2004114985

Printed in Canada

For Catherine Missouri
Now ten
Heart of my hearts
Soul of my soul
May the American republic recover
In time for you to enjoy the bloom.

Everything I do is for you.

ACKNOWLEDGEMENTS

EVERETT ALBERS taught me to project Jefferson into a world he did not live to see without letting my own politics or opinions distort the lens. Ev, who died on August 24, 2004, taught me how to be a public humanities scholar. In giving me the gift of Thomas Jefferson, he changed my life for good.

Bill Chrystal, though an Adamsite and an Augustinian, has spent the past decade exploring these ideas with me on the twenty-second floor of the New Enlightenment Radio Network tower.

Janie Guill made it all happen.

Erin McGee of Iowa provided graphic design and uncommon friendship. She has shown that the art of epistolary communication is not dead in an electronic age.

My dear friend Annie Hall has provided me with paintings of my beloved alter egos, Thomas Jefferson and Theodore Roosevelt. The dapper Halls, Wes and Annie, have provided that most Jeffersonian of all gifts: unalloyed friendship. I cannot thank them enough.

Cathilea Robinett, Susan Sweetland, Dennis McKenna, and Barbara Fulton gave me the forum to work out my ideas. They are Jeffersonians all—the most impressive foursome that I have ever encountered.

Jeffersonians: Lillian Crook, Jim Fuglie, Rachel Retterath, Quentin Hope, Lon From, Kate Magruder, Wendy Raney, Myron Just, Cris Kling, Amy Mazza, John Williams.

Shana Lopez provided the quiet space that enabled me to do the reading that formed the basis of this book.

I owe my own dream of America to my grandparents Rhoda and Dick Straus, who exemplified Jeffersonian values on their modest dairy farm in Fergus Falls, Minnesota; to Mike Jacobs, then a reporter for the Dickinson Press, who taught me why family agriculture is only partly about food production, and who believed the world can be made new through education and revolution; and to Thomas Clayton of that land grant Mecca, the University of Minnesota, who insisted that it is all about lucidity.

The most Jeffersonian person I ever met was Carl Sagan. He showed me the difference between a dilettante and a true Renaissance man.

CONTENTS

How to Use this Book

I am persuaded myself that the good sense of the people will always be found to be the best army. They may be led astray for a moment, but will soon correct themselves. The people are the only censors of their governors; and even their errors will tend to keep these to the true principles of their institution. To punish these errors too severely would be to suppress the only safeguard of the public liberty. The way to prevent these irregular interpositions of the people, is to give them full information of their affairs through the channel of the public papers, and to contrive that those papers should penetrate the whole mass of the people. The basis of our governments being the opinion of the people, the very first object should be to keep that right; and were it left to me to decide whether we should have a government without newspapers, or newspapers without a government, I should not hesitate a moment to prefer the latter.

Jefferson to Edward Carrington
January 16, 1787

How to Use this Book

I WROTE this slender book to encourage a national conversation about the future of America.

Like hundreds of thousands, perhaps millions, of others, I deplore the shallowness, corruption, and frivolousness of our national politics, the puniness of our national attention span, and the inanity of what passes for popular culture in the United States at the beginning of the twenty-first century. It squares not at all with what I learned in civics classes in my youth, nor with the idealism that I felt (and was made to feel) as a child growing up in America in the 1960s and 70s. For all of their childish partisanship, our two national political parties are virtually identical in essential respects. They are, in my view, both Hamiltonian parties: the greater Hamiltonian party and the lesser Hamiltonian party. Nor is it clear that our "official" constitutional culture really governs the United States. From a Jeffersonian point of view, we are in the midst of a fundamental national crisis—and yet we seem not to be talking about it in any meaningful way.

The sorry state we have descended into has produced widespread cynicism and apathy. It is almost impossible to convince anyone that the people of the United States still govern themselves in any meaningful sense, or that our representatives want to do the right thing, or that their actions would make a difference even if they were committed to the commonwealth. There is a very widespread belief that things are bad and that they are going to get worse, not better.

Surely a once-great republic deserves better than this.

I was trained in the public humanities arena as represented by the National Endowment for the Humanities and its state affiliates (partners, they now like to be called), National Public Radio, and public television. My great mentor, Everett C. Albers of the North Dakota Humanities Council, taught me that it is a mistake to conclude that the American people are as shallow and disengaged as they might seem to be. Everett believed—and after addressing public audiences thousands of times, I agree that the American people are intelligent, sensible, concerned about their world, and hungry for intelligent discourse, and that they would respond favorably to more humanities discussions if they were offered in attractive ways. If this is true—that beneath the surface cynicism there is substantial and widespread willingness to engage in a national conversation about the future—then it is of some urgency that we find vehicles and forums for that conversation. This book invites us to dream again about a Jeffersonian republic.

In calling for a national conversation, I have in mind a range of activities, not all of which require the entire population to be engaged at the same time. If everyone who reads this book will initiate discussions of America's identity and place in the world at the workplace water cooler, with his or her spouse and family, among close friends while waiting in line at the restaurant or the movie, in e-mail with one's faraway friends, on the bus, while walking the dog, or while taking a postprandial walk, the dialogue might spread until it embraced a substantial percentage of the American public. I also urge you to host dinner parties for your friends and colleagues, and during them to initiate thoughtful conversations which resemble the salon culture that Jefferson found so satisfying during his Paris years. Raise these questions in church, with your book club, in classrooms, and during sojourns in nature. Put these questions to the politicians who venture into your midst to ask for your support. Write letters to the editor. Post your thoughts on the World Wide Web.

It may be that at some point these local conversations will coalesce into a coordinated national conversation. That would be useful, but it would present severe challenges to the integrity of the conversation. The future of the free world cannot be settled in soundbites between commercials for diet soda and cars and "Girls Gone Wild" videos. But national media attention, however inadequate, might inspire more individuals and groups to undertake the right kind of conversation in Jeffersonian pockets throughout the country. In other words, the conversation can be "national" without having to be conducted on *Larry King Live*.

In a sense, such a discussion would amount to the generational constitutional convention that Jefferson advocated. Jefferson argued that no single generation should fail to re-invent America, to raise the fundamental questions of civilization, and to create its own civic arrangements. Jefferson believed that a nation that governs itself according to an ancient and venerable constitution was almost certainly hidebound and at odds with the actual dynamics of civilization. As the twenty-first century begins, we need to ask ourselves who we are, what we stand for, what we care about, how we would like to be perceived by our friends and enemies, what role we should play in the world, and how we would like to organize our public spaces.

Ideally, the result of such a national conversation would be that a new political party, or at least political persuasion, would rise spontaneously from the sovereign—the American people—and displace the sordid enterprise that passes for our national political culture. Because there is no true alternative to the center-right way things operate under our two-party system, countless Americans have become disaffected, disillusioned, and I think literally diseased. The people need a new vehicle for their idealism, and a new voice for their concerns about their beloved country.

In writing this book, I have no delusions of grandeur or fantasy that it will have profound influence. But I do believe that the first steps toward national renewal must take place soon or we will be beyond redemption. And even if such conversations do not change the course of human events, they certainly will change individual lives. This book is designed to inspire my fellow citizens to become Jeffersonians and to help create a new Jeffersonianism in America. It is my conviction that everyone who leads a more Jeffersonian life will be more fulfilled, happier, more productive, and more influential. I also believe that people who become Jeffersonians because they wish to live well turn out—as if by magic—to be the natural leaders in all the walks of their lives. We seek the Jeffersonian persuasion in our private pursuit of happiness, but it has important and wholly positive social ramifications.

I have attempted here to explore what a Jeffersonian outlook might be at the beginning of the twenty-first century.

Those who are looking for a balanced assessment of Jefferson's strengths and weaknesses will not find it here. I have written about these questions elsewhere. This book emphasizes Jefferson's idealism, his republicanism, his commitment to reason and good sense, and his life as a Renaissance man and an exemplar of the Enlightenment. In other words, this book emphasizes Jefferson's positive vision for the American republic.

I do not wish to be perceived as somehow "in denial" about the dark side of Jefferson's life and character. I am fully aware that Jefferson was a slaveowner, a racist, an apartheidist, a perpetuator of slavery into the American West, and (probably) the father of several of Sally Hemings' children. I know that Jefferson advocated Indian removal policies that barely distinguish him from his successor Andrew Jackson, and that there were times, admittedly few, when he fantasized about the extinction of at least some portions of Indian America. I realize that Jefferson had a patronizing attitude toward women in public life, and that his preference for women who exhibited "that softness of disposition which is the ornament of her sex & charm of ours,"[1] has a grating effect on enlightened men and women of our time. I know that some historians regard Jefferson's intensely selfish relationships with his two adult daughters as psychologically claustrophobic, and arguably worse. I know that Jefferson was a profligate spender who died helplessly in debt. I know, too, that Jefferson had a Machiavellian streak that led him to fight unscrupulously to defeat his enemies in the Federalist Party between 1790 and 1800, and that this included paying James Callender to write ugly nonsense about the Adams administration. I know that Jefferson can be shown to have (at one time or another) advocated prosecution of opposition newspapers, censorship, and an erosion of the fourth amendment;

1. To Maria Cosway, October 12, 1786.

that he prejudiced the Aaron Burr treason trial; and that he wrote a bill of attainder while serving as the wartime governor of Virginia. There is more. And it is not admirable.

By now it is clear to everyone that the man Thomas Jefferson was not always equal to the ideals he so beautifully espoused. We are witnessing the ex post facto tragedy of Thomas Jefferson, for the definition of tragedy is that a great individual is destroyed not by impersonal forces of destiny, but by unresolved energies in his own character. The fall of Thomas Jefferson poses a twofold danger to our republic. First, some have come to refuse to listen to Jefferson because they cannot stomach what they perceive to be his inconsistencies or (as extremists put it) his contemptible hypocrisies. They have stopped listening to Jefferson's Enlightenment pronouncements, because they cannot help but deconstruct them in light of Jefferson's some-times deplorable actual behavior in the world. Second, and much worse, some believe that the ideals that Jefferson espoused are inherently problematic, even meaningless, and that Jefferson's profound inconsisten-cies signify not just the measure of his personal failures, but the essential hollowness of his ideals, or for that matter any Enlightenment ideals.

This seems to me to be the veriest nonsense. The Enlightenment's ideals, for all of their seeming superfi-ciality, have revolutionized the world and bettered life on earth in undeniable and measurable ways. No people who enjoys the fruits of the Enlightenment—the rule of law, secular education, bills of rights, separation of church and state, the sanctity of contract, the apotheosis of science, free press, and free enquiry—would ever choose to go back to something more fundamentalist.

Jefferson was closer to the Enlightenment's ideals than most people of his time. Some of his friends and heroes were closer to those ideals than Jefferson. Those ideals matter, and when we are our best selves, and when America is its best self, those ideals inspire the entire world with their breathtaking clarity and dignity. If Jefferson is now perceived to have failed, we are free to judge him and even dismiss him personally, but the ideals that he espoused will continue to be the standard of personal character, the pursuit of happiness, and the purposes of civilization forever. Jefferson knew this. His willingness to articulate the universal from within the "too too solid world" of actual life in eighteenth-century Virginia (or Philadelphia or Paris) is in fact the foundation of his greatness.

I believe that the United States needs a new infusion of what might be called clarified (or updated) Jeffersonianism. At the very least, we need a new generation of Jeffersonians.

This book is my modest attempt to define and inspire that national conversation.

Clay S. Jenkinson
Marmarth, North Dakota

A Jeffersonian Renewal for America
A Call for a Second American Enlightenment

> What a stupendous, what an incomprehensible machine is man! who can endure toil, famine, stripes, imprisonment, and death itself in vindication of his own liberty, and the next moment be deaf to all those motives whose power supported him through his trial and inflict on his fellow men a bondage one hour of which is fraught with more misery than ages of that which he rose in rebellion to oppose.
>
> Jefferson to de Meusnier
> June 1786

A Jeffersonian Renewal for America
A Call for a Second American Enlightenment

JEFFERSON HAS been dead since July 4, 1826. He lived on the other side of the industrial revolution, the other side of the Civil War, the other side of the emergence of the United States as a world power, the other side of the Marxist and Freudian divides, on the other side of the Civil Rights Acts of 1964 and 1965, and the other side of the pell-mell peopling of the American continent in the nineteenth and twentieth centuries. Some of what he believed (the possible racial inferiority of African-Americans, the primarily domestic destiny of women) has been resoundingly discredited. Many of his ideas made sense in his own time and place, when, in Jefferson's terms, the continent appeared to be a vast tabula rasa waiting to be inscribed with whatever civilization the American people could agree to create, but those same ideas are harder to maintain now that we have become an urban-industrial, consumerist, world empire. Jefferson's profound agrarianism, for example, is still perceived by many as the path the American people ought to have taken, but since we did not take that path, there is little point in pretending that a nation of family farmers is still a possibility.

The last thing Jefferson would have wanted would be to be remembered as the champion of lost causes. Jefferson was a flexible visionary, a dynamic rather than a static thinker, and he preferred to envision the future rather than cling to the ways of the past. One of his mottos was *nil desperandum*, nothing is to be despaired of in America, and we are never to permit ourselves to be enslaved by the artifices of civilization.

It is certain that stupendous advances in our technologies—from refrigeration and automobiles to the World Wide Web and the electronic economy—have worked revolutionary changes in American civilization, and that these changes render many of Jefferson's ways and ideas inapplicable to our lives at the beginning of the twenty-first century. For example, the Founding Fathers (particularly the author of the Second Amendment, the cautious and pacific James Madison) would probably think differently about guns at a time when an uninformed, uneducated, uncivil, and unsupervised individual with crack in his veins and a chip on his shoulder can possess a weapon that fires one hundred bullets in less than a minute.

With a modicum of careful reading, it is possible to determine what the historical figure Thomas Jefferson (1743-1826) believed. He was, after all, both prolific and astonishingly articulate. It is more fruitful, and more challenging, to try to determine what Jefferson might make of our world, and what parts of his vision of America are still applicable two hundred years later.

So what endures of a *Jeffersonian* worldview at the beginning of the twenty-first century? Acknowledging the obvious fact that we are no longer a pre-industrial nation with a small and relatively homogenous population, and that Jefferson would have been the least likely of the Founding Fathers to cling to the systems of his own time and place, how does a modern Jeffersonian see the world? That is the purpose of this book.

Self-Reliance

If you always lean on your master, you will never be able to proceed without him. It is a part of the American character to consider nothing as desperate; to surmount every difficulty by resolution and contrivance. In Europe there are shops for every want; its inhabitants, therefore, have no idea that their wants can be supplied otherwise. Remote from all other aid, we are obliged to invent and to execute; to find means within ourselves, and not to lean on others.

Jefferson to Martha Jefferson,
Aix en Provence, March 28th, 1787

Self-Reliance

FIRST, a Jeffersonian believes in self-reliance. We may not be able to subsist outside of Hamiltonian institutions any longer, but every Jeffersonian American is aware of how morally and politically compromising it is to be so dependent on transnational corporations, foreign resources, and centralized government for our daily survival. Good Jeffersonians understand their technical, political, and moral relationship to the grids that deliver their food, shelter, electricity, fuel, clothing, and gadgets. An understanding of the supply lines of our civilization is in itself liberating because knowledge is always preferable to ignorance, and an understanding of the ways systems work at least invites the possibility of action (and liberation) rather than passivity. A Jeffersonian resists the dependencies of modern life, at least in some symbolic way.

Jeffersonians grow something: raise some of their own food perhaps, if only a few tomatoes or pears; plant flowers in a window box; nurture a few vines and perhaps press a few grapes. Jefferson was certain that placing one's hands in the earth was one of the keys to humility and human happiness.

Perhaps we cannot, like Jefferson, dance the minuet, read Homer and Plutarch in the original Greek, design a Palladian villa, invent a revolutionary plow, and write a state paper of global importance, but a Jeffersonian attempts to cultivate a range of practical life skills that signify the will to achieve independence. A Jeffersonian takes pride in knowing how to do things: weld, perhaps, or plumb, bind books, fire a kiln, change the oil, build a desk, sew, quilt, make jelly, design a website, or perhaps build a telescope.

In the face of the dependencies and structural degradations of modern life, these are of course merely symbolic declarations of independence, but the Jeffersonian undertakes them because each gesture of independence invites the next, and each tends to build confidence in the proposition that we become more completely human to the extent that we replace a money economy with one based upon competence and gumption.

The great Jeffersonians get off the grid to the extent possible without becoming silly or primitive. There are Jeffersonians who produce their own water and power supplies, who build their own houses, and who live with minimal contact with the internal combustion engine and its vast enabling infrastructure. These last free men and women are to be admired if not actually imitated because, in Jefferson's words, they "keep alive that sacred fire which otherwise might disappear from the earth."

Foreign Policy

I am for relying, for internal defence, on our militia solely, till actual invasion, and for such a naval force only as may protect our coasts and harbors from such depredations as we have experienced; and not for a standing army in time of peace, which may overawe the public sentiment; nor for a navy, which, by its own expenses and the eternal wars in which it will implicate us, will grind us with public burthens, and sink us under them. I am for free commerce with all nations; political connection with none; and little or no diplomatic establishment. And I am not for linking ourselves by new treaties with the quarrels of Europe; entering that field of slaughter to preserve their balance, or joining in the confederacy of kings to war against the principles of liberty.

Jefferson to Elbridge Gerry
January 26, 1799

Foreign Policy

SECOND, a Jeffersonian has a very modest idea of America's place in the world. As the twenty-first century begins, and in the wake of the September 11, 2001 catastrophes, the United States cannot permit itself to want to be isolationist any longer, but we can still honor Jefferson's principle that our best export is the Idea of America: that we should mind our own business as much as possible; build a nation just, equal, beautiful, and culturally remarkable; and then quietly invite the rest of the world to become enamored of our model and our success. Jefferson believed that the United States had no duty or right to police the world. In fact, he believed that "entangling alliances" with the nations of the Old World could only sully the purity of the republican experiment in America.

Jefferson understood that each country has its own history, tradition, and social dynamic, and that it would be naïve and arrogant to believe that American-style democracy can be transferred intact from the United States to other nations. Asked by Lafayette and others to advise the French people in the midst of their great revolution (1789-1799), Jefferson surprised (and disappointed) his hosts by suggesting that the French people adopt a conservative rather than a radical new constitution. He warned that if France tried to leap ahead too fast, and without adequate education of the French masses, the revolution might end in a military dictatorship—which it did.

Jefferson is one of the originators of the idea of American exceptionalism, the conviction that the American experiment is fundamentally different from that of the history and destiny of other nations, that what worked for Europe will not necessarily work here, and what works here will not very likely translate to social and demographic conditions elsewhere.

Jefferson would surely argue that our duty is to study the world, master the geography, economics, and political arrangements of the planet, and appreciate the diversity of the world's social arrangements, rather than attempt to impose a monocultural pattern of political and economic development on nations with a fundamentally different history. It is hard to believe that Jefferson could support regime change, pre-emptive strikes, weapons of mass destruction, or the idea that dependence on foreign resources like oil could be construed to constitute an American "interest" in another sovereign nation or a region of the planet.

The course of human events over the past century (from McKinley to the Bush dynasty) has forced the United States to take seriously its place in the larger world. Without ever quite talking it through, the United States ceased to be a republic and became an empire during the twentieth century. If, in the wake of September 11, 2001, the United States is—like it or not—a central player in the troubled theater of the world, we can still be Jeffersonians if we:

- bring Enlightenment idealism to our relations with the other peoples of the world;

- believe in the rule of law, and the need to subordinate force to law and negotiation wherever possible, even when that course proves exceedingly frustrating;

- approach the rest of the world with humility, with curiosity, with deep study, and with tolerance;

- understand that each nation, tribe, or culture has its own traditions, history, habits, and spirit, and that it is not for us to pretend that all peoples want to live like us: buy what we buy, watch what we watch, speak as we speak, or subordinate the life of the spirit as we do to the pursuit of material happiness;

- realize that while economic activity and prosperity are important, the purpose of the world is not profit and power, but culture, dignity, and liberty;

- realize that in a world where national boundaries have been eroded by the forces of globalization, the need for distributive justice now applies to peoples throughout regions, even throughout the world, not just to citizens of a single nation state. In a global village characterized by intense electronic networking, until there is some equalization of the distribution of the basic fruits of life (food, shelter, basic clothing, medical care), we can expect anger, violence, illegal immigration, terrorism, and war.

In every government on earth is some trace of human weakness, some germ of corruption and degeneracy, which cunning will discover and wickedness insensibly open, cultivate, and improve. Every government degenerates when trusted to the rulers of the people alone. The people themselves therefore are its only safe depositories. And to render even them safe, their minds must be improved to a certain degree.

Jefferson, *Notes on the State of Virginia*

Education

A **JEFFERSONIAN** believes in the Archimedean power of education and—in spite of all the evidence—continues to be the champion of the public education system in the United States. Jefferson warned us that we could not be a nation ignorant and free. No honest person can deny our national ignorance as the twenty-first century begins. We are today the most ill-educated great nation in the world, indeed the most ill-educated great nation in human history. Jefferson believed that in a republic every individual needs to be educated up to his or her capacity. The widespread anti-intellectual streak in the American character would have seemed to Jefferson not only self-defeating, but the death knell of anything like an American republic.

Suspicious of positive government (the welfare state), Jefferson believed that education is the panacea, that almost all social ills will disappear in a better informed and better educated nation. In the face of all the perceived problems of American life, Jefferson would almost certainly argue that education is the answer to each one of them, infinitely preferable to regulation, taxation, reparation, or the appropriation of money for new applications of the welfare state.

For Jefferson, education is not merely book learning. Although he was one of the best educated men in American history, Jefferson was a thoroughgoing pragmatist who believed that the practical arts (such as agriculture, seamanship, and craftwork) were every bit as important as political theory or Greek grammar. Jefferson was the founder of the University of Virginia, but he is also considered the father of the community and junior college system, vocational education, and (with Dr. Franklin) public libraries. Theory and metaphysics frustrated him. He embodied the spirit of the American Philosophical Society, which was dedicated to the promotion of useful knowledge.

Jefferson considered his father Peter's desire that he be fully and classically educated to be more important than any material inheritance he might have received. He was committed to lifelong learning, and he seems to have believed not that education is a preparation for life, but that it is a way of life in an enlightened world, especially in a society that has committed itself to self-government. The Jeffersonian is a severe autodidact who looks upon the years of formal education merely as a foundation for the decades of hard study and reading that almost alone redeem life from its tedium and its many social and biological setbacks.

Jefferson was not in any way hostile to private education, but he would be rigidly antagonistic to the idea of spending public money to support private education. Jefferson sought to maintain a wall of separation between public and private ventures (the burden in public ventures is accessibility and equality), and he believed that the public school was a kind of miniature laboratory of democracy, where the children of rich and poor, Jew and gentile, farmer and merchant, genius and plodder met under conditions of mutual respect and tolerance.

Leadership

The ground of liberty is to be gained by inches, that we must be contented to secure what we can get from time to time, and eternally press forward for what is yet to get. It takes time to persuade men to do even what is for their own good.

Jefferson to Charles Clay, January 27, 1790

Truth advances, & error recedes step by step only; and to do to our fellow-men the most good in our power, we must lead where we can, follow where we cannot, and still go with them, watching always the favorable moment for helping them to another step.

Jefferson to Thomas Cooper, October 7, 1814

My great wish is to go on in a strict but silent performance of my duty: to avoid attracting notice & to keep my name out of newspapers, because I find the pain of a little censure, even when it is unfounded, is more acute than the pleasure of much praise.

Jefferson to Francis Hopkinson, March 12, 1789

Leadership

A **JEFFERSONIAN** is a natural, albeit reluctant leader. Although he preferred to be home at Monticello among his gardens, grandchildren, orchards, and books, Jefferson held nearly every office available in the United States in his time. Reluctant though he was, he was the master leader of his generation, and he managed somehow to stay afloat through forty years of one of the most tempestuous times in American political history. Meanwhile, the two Adamses were confined to single terms, Washington had lost a good deal of national support by the time he retired, and Madison and Monroe would probably not have become President were it not for the prior leadership of Jefferson. Hamilton was unelectable and Patrick Henry remained a Virginia statesman. Jefferson alone bestrode the early national period like a colossus.

Jefferson was a mild-mannered leader who steadfastly refused to call attention to himself. He preferred to work by indirection. He shrank from conflicts, or at least had lieutenants handle them on his behalf, so that he could maintain his characteristic repose. Jefferson's leadership style consisted of:

- profound clarity of expression;
- mastery of detail—he was always the best prepared person in the room;
- optimism;
- personal generosity and sympathy;
- advocacy of the people's rights, dignity, and capacity for self-government;
- steady and respectful communication with everyone he wanted to persuade.

Jefferson was not just a leader in the political arena. He was a leader in architecture, in agriculture, in science, and in literature. He seems really to have believed that the leader's duty was to "ameliorate the condition of mankind," with as little fanfare as possible, and calling as little attention to himself as possible.

Leadership is a paradoxical entity in a republic. If we believe that the people are capable of governing themselves with little or no top-down coordination, little room is left for leadership in any traditional sense. Republican leaders are (seemingly?) egoless men like Jefferson, rather than heroes on horseback like Theodore Roosevelt. Jefferson prided himself on always adhering to two principles: that the rational, enlightened path is always preferable to one based on traditional assertions of power; and that it is rarely, if ever, a good idea to thwart the decided will of the people.

Jeffersonians provide leadership because they know that if the exemplars of reason and good sense abdicate their public responsibilities, the advocates of force and social hierarchy will run away with the country. They lead because they know that the world becomes more enlightened only if every enlightened person gives energy to the commonwealth energies of the community. Jeffersonians lead because they know that social apathy is not an option in a republic.

Like the master, Jeffersonians lead by suavity, the arts of rational persuasion, indirection, and a commitment to social harmony. They master whatever they undertake. They perennially keep in mind the desired outcome, not the primacy of their own egos. They are modest about their accomplishments and they are reluctant to stand at the front of any group whatsoever.

Distributive Justice

The property of this country [France] is absolutely concentrated in a very few hands . . . The consequences of this enormous inequality producing so much misery to the bulk of mankind, legislators cannot invent too many devices for subdividing property. . . . Whenever there is in any country uncultivated lands and unemployed poor, it is clear that the laws of property have been so far extended as to violate natural right. The earth is given as a common stock for man to labor and live on. If for the encouragement of industry we allow it to be apportioned, we must take care that other employment be provided to those excluded from the appropriation. If we do not, the fundamental right to labor the earth returns to the unemployed.

Jefferson to Rev. James Madison
October 28, 1785

Distributive Justice

A JEFFERSONIAN believes that the economy, left to itself, distributes the fruits of life unfairly, that a just society has no choice but to find ways to limit the excesses of capitalism, and indeed to be prepared to redistribute wealth to a certain degree in the name of equality of circumstance. This is something of a paradox, because Jefferson did not like government, and he certainly did not believe in the set of government programs that are embraced by the terms New Deal, welfare state, or Great Society. How does a suspicious libertarian, a disciple of Adam Smith, prevent the excesses of runaway capitalism?

Jefferson hoped that American circumstances would somehow magically discourage severe inequalities in the distribution of wealth. But if unjustifiable concentrations of wealth did occur, Jefferson's reluctant solution was a graduated income tax that would serve as a disincentive to vast accumulations of wealth and would make funds available for some sort of benign redistribution downward to the less fortunate individuals of American society. Think of Sweden, perhaps, with severely graduated income taxes, but without the welfare state.

At the very least Jefferson believed that we must all agree that great differentials in wealth and material comfort are not an inevitable and therefore acceptable fact of life. Jefferson regarded disproportionate accumulations of wealth as a socially derived privilege rather than a natural right of property, and he believed that we must all acknowledge, as part of our social contract, that when the gap between rich and poor gets to be too large, we have a commonwealth interest in making careful adjustments in the name of fairness.

The assumption of the conservatives of our time, that the rich deserve what they have and the poor are simply not working hard enough, would strike Jefferson as a weak-minded apology for pseudo-aristocracy and economic corruption. Like his hero John Locke, Jefferson believed that every individual has a natural right to a farm or its economic equivalent; that humans are born with the basic right to subsistence, provided that they are willing to work to achieve it; and that any economic system that forgets this fact is a corrupt one. Jefferson believed that while the enlightened state ought to be reluctant to interfere in the free workings of the economy, at the very least it must not lend its official energies to the protection and promotion of artificial privilege. In other words, the enlightened state errs on the side of equality rather than wealth. Jefferson believed that education was the great equalizer—that if we educated everyone to his capacity, the middle class would grow almost to the end of the spectrum on both sides (extreme wealth and extreme poverty), and that the problem of maldistribution of wealth would diminish, if not completely disappear. Jefferson believed that property was important but not sacrosanct.

When young any composition pleases which unites a little sense, some imagination, and some rhythm, in doses however small. But as we advance in life these things fall off one by one, and I suspect we are left at last with only Homer and Virgil, perhaps with Homer alone.

To read the Latin and Greek authors in their original is a sublime luxury; and I deem luxury in science to be at least as justifiable as in architecture, painting, gardening, or the other arts. I enjoy Homer in his own language infinitely beyond Pope's translation of him. . . . I thank on my knees him who directed my early education for having put into my possession this rich source of delight; and I would not exchange it for anything which I could then have acquired, and have not since acquired.

Jefferson to Joseph Priestley
January 27, 1800

Love of Books

A JEFFERSONIAN believes that books are at the center of any full and mature life. Thomas Jefferson approached life essentially through books. He obtained between seven and ten thousand of them in the course of his lifetime, at a time when books were rare and extremely expensive. Reading was one of his favorite activities. He prepared himself for adult life with the severest possible course of reading. For a significant period of his life, from about the age of fifteen to twenty-five, Jefferson essentially read every waking minute of every day. With the possible exceptions of Theodore Roosevelt and John Quincy Adams, Jefferson was intellectually the best-prepared president in American history.

Jefferson believed in the good sense of the American people, that no matter what their educational attainments, the mass of people would always exhibit enough good sense to govern themselves intelligently. But he knew, too, that the great texts of western civilization provide indispensable clues about the ways to achieve and preserve human liberty, not to mention happiness. History not only teaches us what bad government has been, but how to use the sad record of the past to envision and fight for a more enlightened future. To John Brazier, Jefferson wrote, "It is often said there have been shining examples of men of great abilities, in all businesses of life, without any other science [i.e. knowledge] than what they had gathered from conversation and intercourse with the world. But, who can say what these men would not have been, had they started in the science on the shoulders of a Demosthenes or Cicero, of a Locke, or Bacon, or a Newton?"[2]

2. To John Brazier, August 14, 1819.

Jefferson's reading habits were eclectic, but he clearly preferred non-fiction, and his immense library was essentially a reference collection. What Jefferson wanted most were information, facts, data points, and statistics. He saw books primarily as information delivery systems. He would be pleased at the size, scope, and accessibility of the public library system in the United States, and thrilled at the World Wide Web and the Internet.

Even so, Jefferson loved books as books, and regarded them as sensuous objects, and even works of art. He made sure that his beloved books were elegantly and sumptuously bound, shelved in aesthetic good taste, and classified intelligently. Unlike his disputatious friend John Adams, Jefferson did not deface his books with hectic scribbling. His marginalia were confined to careful correction of spelling and grammar in the volumes he accumulated. He loved fine (expensive) paper, good ink, and handsome typography. On average, books were in Jefferson's time dramatically more pleasant to hold and caress and pore over than the books of our time. When Jefferson said he could not live without books, he meant it. It is just so with Jeffersonians.

Jefferson could not have agreed with Robert Louis Stevenson: "Books are good enough in their own way, but they are a mighty bloodless substitute for life."

The Role of Government

With all these blessings, what more is necessary to make us a happy and prosperous people? Still one thing more, fellow-citizens—a wise and frugal government which shall restrain men from injuring one another, which shall leave them otherwise free to regulate their own pursuits of industry and improvement, and shall not take from the mouth of labor the bread it has earned. This is the sum of good government, and this is necessary to close the circle of our felicities.

Jefferson, First Inaugural Address
March 4, 1801

The Role of Government

A JEFFERSONIAN believes that government exists solely to fulfill the will of the people, that we need less rather than more of it, that citizens need to be eternally vigilant if they wish to retain their liberties, and that good citizens flare up whenever they sense that government is failing to represent their interests. Jeffersonians are suspicious of government in general and they assume that any particular government is probably up to no good. A Jeffersonian is a prickly, and at times a crabby, citizen. Government officials are not seen as remarkable beings deserving of special respect, and certainly not majestic in any way, but rather servants of the people who need to be reminded with some frequency that they exist merely to perform tasks on behalf of their sovereign masters, the people. Any pretension to regal status, any expression of arrogance or gubernatorial independence, is swiftly and severely punished.

Jefferson did not see government as a purveyor of blessings. He would have been appalled by the welfare state, first because it necessitates large government and presumes that a single government can ascertain what a large, diverse, and geographically dispersed population needs, and second because it undermines the self-reliance of the citizenry and encourages individuals to abdicate responsibility while looking instead to government for their well-being.

In Jefferson's formulation, citizens are entitled under natural law, if they wish, to govern themselves directly in genuine democracy—every citizen gathering periodically in the agora or public square. Because direct democracy is inconvenient, especially over long distances and for large populations, citizens agree to engage public agents, called representatives, to do their bidding in the public square. These representatives are like proxy agents at a public auction. They do not have the authority to make independent decisions. They do the bidding of their citizens in a faithful, even literalist, way, and on those few occasions when they deviate from what Jefferson called "the decided choice"[3] of their constituents, they candidly volunteer the truth about their actions, without attempting to evade responsibility, and they invite the citizens to retire them to private life if they are offended by decisions made without their direct authorization. When Jefferson purchased the Louisiana territory in 1803 contrary to his own constitutional theory, he noted that he had done what a guardian might do for his ward, and that the ward was entitled to repudiate the actions of the guardian, in which case the guardian "must get out of the scrape as I can."[4]

This was Jefferson's understanding of the principle of self-government and the will of the people. In practice he was inevitably more flexible, especially when he and his Republican friends were in power. The "logic" of this increased confidence was that he believed that he and his friends were in tune with the people in a way that the arrogant Federalists could never be.

People who call themselves Jeffersonians today are much less literal about representation and the will of the people. They are more concerned with the general tenor of government activity, and they routinely entrust their representatives with more freedom of action than would have satisfied Jefferson, in or out of power. There is widespread acceptance nowadays of the idea that average citizens cannot be expected to keep up

3. To John Jay, August 23, 1785.
4. To John Breckenridge, August 12, 1803.

with the workings of government and the complex world it represents, and that the will of the people is a general will, not a bill of particulars. Jefferson would have understood this, given the size and complexity of our social fabric, but he would not have liked it. Government in the twenty-first century is inevitably more detached from the will of the people than it was in Jefferson's time, or in his constitutional theory. Perhaps all that can now be expected of a Jeffersonian is that she or he remember that government is intended to be tethered in some dynamic way to the will of the people, that government is not a management team given broad powers to make the corporation prosper.

The Size of Government

Were it made a question, whether no law, as among the savage Americans, or too much law, as among the civilized Europeans, submits man to the greatest evil, one who has seen both conditions of existence would pronounce it to be the last; and that the sheep are happier of themselves, than under care of the wolves. It will be said, the great societies cannot exist without government. The savages, therefore, break them into small ones.

Jefferson, *Notes on the State of Virginia*

The Size of Government

A JEFFERSONIAN believes in minimal government. In his own time, Jefferson advocated a tiny,
almost non-existent national government (he actually
called it the "foreign department"[5]); somewhat more
energetic state governments; and still more emphatic
local governments, his cherished Anglo-Saxon "hundreds" or ward republics. He believed the national
government's portfolio should be strictly limited to the
powers enumerated in the Constitution of the United
States and that the national government should do only
those things that were truly national or international in
scope. At the same time, he believed that government, at
any level, should do only those things that government
alone can accomplish, and that everything else should
be undertaken by individual and private enterprise.
The goal of the national government, Jefferson wrote,
consists of a few plain duties to be performed by a few
honest men. He believed that ambition and careerism
were the death of republican liberty. In theory, at least,
Jefferson declared himself to be a semi-anarchist.

Obviously, a strictly libertarian government is no
longer feasible today, given the urban, industrial,
electronic, military, and chemical complexities of our
civilization. Some people who think of themselves as
"Jeffersonians" argue for a libertarian system, but this
is to pretend that the world of the early twenty-first
century is not fundamentally different from the world
of 1803. A true Jeffersonian envisions a government
as limited as possible, but as energetic as necessary to
accomplish those things that a government must do on
our behalf. In other words, a Jeffersonian is an advocate

5. To Edward Livingston, March 25, 1825.

of governmental restraint, not minimalism, and a champion of volunteerism and individual initiative.

Jefferson advocated minimal government chiefly because he had faith in the individual's ability to craft a life for him or herself, partly because he understood that "the tendency of things is for liberty to yield, and government to gain ground."[6] Although he was no Leninist, he looked forward to a time when formal government would almost disappear altogether, and highly evolved individuals would govern themselves in the profoundest sense of the term. Such dreams as this led Alexander Hamilton to dismiss Jefferson as an "intellectual voluptuary," and John Adams to ask whether he was not perhaps "fast asleep in philosophical tranquility."

Jefferson believed that the history of the world was the story of all the ways in which too much government had spoiled the happiness of peoples and trampled on their rights. Jefferson understood that an upright and well-meaning government was seductively appealing, and that intelligent citizens delude themselves into believing that a government that begins in virtue will never lose sight of its foundational values. Good citizens must force themselves to resist the siren song of the welfare state, because big government soon begins to take citizens for granted, and a government large enough to distribute happiness can just as easily take it away when that becomes more convenient.

Jefferson's governmental minimalism is a source of genuine frustration for modern Jeffersonians—for two reasons. First, Jeffersonians have come to be very fond of certain government programs, knowing full well that the master would have regarded them with suspicion. The Jefferson who told his close friend Charles Wilson Peale that he could not support a national museum,

6. To Edward Carrington, May 27, 1788.

however desirable, without an enabling amendment to the U.S. Constitution, would undoubtedly frown on federally funded public television and public radio, the national endowments for the arts and humanities, the national galleries, perhaps even the Smithsonian and the National Science Foundation. All Jeffersonians prize such agencies. Jefferson would probably have found them disturbing, no matter how much he enjoyed or contributed to their programs.

Second, most Jeffersonians are now convinced that the national government is more enlightened than the states and individual communities, and they look to the national government to deliver Jeffersonian goods by—well—Hamiltonian means (big and expensive government programs, and central authority and initiative). They see government as a tool of justice and social progress, and they tend to find Jefferson's minimalism both quaint and embarrassing.

It is at least possible that even Jefferson, had he seen the complexities of the world in which we find ourselves, might have come to terms with a stronger and more pro-active national government. But it is not a good idea to assume that he could have made such a revolutionary adjustment in his core political philosophy or that he would be as tolerant of Hamiltonian nationalism as his well-meaning heirs tend to be. The most faithful Jeffersonian attitude would seem to be a consistently skeptical approach to any program, legislation, or initiative that increases the size of government, requires a permanent infusion of tax revenue, or swells the scope, depth, energy, or dignity of government. The Jeffersonian perennially asks, "However useful, convenient, or appealing this government function may appear to be, do we truly need it, and is there not some private—or at least more local—way to accomplish the same thing?"

Like my friend the Doctor, I have lived temperately, eating little animal food, and that not as an aliment, so much as a condiment for the vegetables, which constitute my principal diet. I double however, the Doctor's glass and a half of wine, and even treble it with a friend; but halve its effects by drinking the weak wines only. The ardent wines I cannot drink, nor do I use ardent spirits in any form. Malt liquors and cider are my table drinks, and my breakfast, like that also of my friend, is of tea and coffee. I have been blest with organs of digestion which accept and concoct, without ever murmuring, whatever the palate chooses to consign to them; and I have not yet lost a tooth by age. I was a hard student until I entered on the business of life, the duties of which leave no idle time to those disposed to fulfil them; and now, retired, and at` the age of seventy-six, I am again a hard student. Indeed, my fondness for reading and study revolts me from the drudgery of letter-writing. And a stiff wrist, the consequence of an early dislocation, makes writing both slow and painful. I am not so regular in my sleep as the Doctor says he was, devoting to it from five to eight hours, according as my company or the book I am reading interests me ; and I never go to bed without an hour, or half hour's previous reading of something moral, whereon to ruminate in the intervals of sleep. But whether I retire to bed early or late, I rise with the sun. I use spectacles at night, but not necessarily in the day, unless in reading small print. My hearing is distinct in particular conversation, but confused when several voices cross each other, which unfits me for the society of the table. I have been more fortunate than my friend in the article of health. So free from catarrhs that I have not had one, (in the breast, I mean) on an average of eight or ten years through life. I ascribe this exemption partly to the habit of bathing my feet in cold water every morning, for sixty years past. A fever of more than twenty-four hours I have not had above two or three times in my life. A periodical headache has afflicted me occasionally, once, perhaps; in six or eight years, for two or three weeks at a time, which seems now to have left me.

Jefferson to Dr. Vine Utley
March 21, 1819

Balance

JEFFERSONIANS ARE pragmatic idealists, and practical utopians. Jefferson's enemies called him "philosopher," "dreamer," and "utopian." He was regarded as a Platonic philosopher, "fast asleep in philosophical tranquility," while more practical men like Madison and John Adams did what they could to anchor him to the real world. And yet Jefferson reformed our coinage, built a university out of brick and marble, created a rectilinear survey grid system that organized our entire western development, and tinkered incessantly with gadgets and labor-saving devices. He had the capacity to state the universal truth on such questions as freedom of the press or the right to revolution, but he had a deep distaste for metaphysics. He dreamed of an American pastoral utopia, but he worked hard to raise funds for a canal that would link the Potomac River to the American interior. He was a fascinating mix of the universal and the concrete. It is never possible to dismiss him as a "utopian," for few dreamers ever accomplished as much.

Jeffersonians know that half a loaf is better than none. They dream of an America in which everyone is educated to her or his capacity, where citizens are eternally vigilant, where science rules, and where people pursue happiness and dignity and the life of the mind rather than storm a new shopping mall on the day of its grand opening. But they also fight to keep *Catcher in the Rye* from being banned by the local school district, and they help to organize day care centers in the workplace. To be a Jeffersonian is to remain an idealist in adult life without being silly or uninformed. Jeffersonians envision a second American Enlightenment, but they also work assiduously to bring about small improvements in the world around them.

In a sense, Jeffersonians work a variation on the great motto, "Think Globally, Act Locally." Jeffersonians dream idealistically, but they act pragmatically. For Jefferson, and for Jeffersonians, this has proved to be an enormously attractive (and powerful) combination of energies. It is virtually the only formula for changing the world gracefully.

Liberty v. Security

It would be a dangerous delusion were a confidence in the man of our choice to silence our fears for the safety of our rights: that confidence is everywhere the parent of despotism—free government is founded in jealousy, and not in confidence; it is jealousy and not confidence which prescribes limited constitutions, to bind down those whom we are obliged to trust with power. . . . In questions of power, then, let no more be heard of confidence in man, but bind him down from mischief by the chains of the Constitution.

Jefferson, *Kentucky Resolutions*, October 1798

Liberty v. Security

A JEFFERSONIAN believes that liberty is more important than security and freedom more important than order. A Jeffersonian world is somewhat disorderly, because the people are tearing up their constitution from time to time, and surging into the public square with their pitchforks every time government exhibits the habits of tyranny. In a letter to his closest confidant James Madison, Jefferson cited the Latin maxim, *Malo periculosam libertatem quam quietem servitutem* [I prefer a dangerous liberty to quiet servitude].[7] Jefferson alone of the Founding Fathers was an apologist for rebellion, revolution, even the French Reign of Terror. He was fond of organic metaphors that likened violent revolution to the routine events of the garden. Most famously, he wrote, "The tree of liberty must be refreshed, from time to time, with the blood of patriots and tyrants. It is its natural manure." It would be impossible to sound more serene about the possibility of mayhem in the streets. This kind of talk led John Adams to ask, "What think you of terrorism, Mr. Jefferson?"

Jefferson cheerfully accepted that liberty is a messy business, that a volatile public, a certain amount of chaos, and even some tyranny of the majority are important (if somewhat inconvenient) signs of the health of a republic. When most of the national establishment was alarmed and offended by Shays' rebellion in western Massachusetts, Jefferson blithely asked his friend William Stephens Smith, "What signify a few lives lost in a century or two?...God forbid we should ever be 20 years without such a rebellion...What country can preserve it's liberties if their rulers are not warned from time to time that their people preserve the

7. To James Madison, January 30, 1787.

spirit of resistance?" And when the French Revolution descended into its bloodiest phase, Jefferson refused to denounce the Reign of Terror. To his protégé William Short he declared, "The liberty of the whole earth was depending on the issue of the contest [the French Revolution], and was ever such a prize won with so little innocent blood? . . . rather than it should have failed, I would have seen half the earth desolated. Were there but an Adam and an Eve left in every country, and left free, it would be better than it now is."[8]

Jefferson believed that government must be kept on the defensive at all times, that the people not only have a natural right to withdraw consent from their social compact, but that they should shake up government from time to time just to remind their governors that they serve at the pleasure of the people and not otherwise. In other words, for the Jeffersonians, liberty is the quintessence of life, and government is a necessary evil.

Jeffersonians should never be more afraid than when government offers to provide increased security by way of increased authority. He surely approved of the adage attributed to Benjamin Franklin: "They that can give up essential liberty to obtain a little temporary safety deserve neither liberty nor safety." Jefferson's attitude would be that national survival and national security are the highest good, of course, but that they must be preserved with the profoundest respect for the Bill of Rights, constitutional legitimacy, and the natural law principle that government should intrude upon our liberties as minimally and as humbly as possible. The Jeffersonian's attitude toward the security state is "prove it." "Prove to me that my well-being depends upon my yielding more of my liberty to the

8. To William Stephens Smith, November 13, 1787; to William Short, January 3, 1793.

state. Prove to me that there is no less onerous way to survive."

Jefferson was aware that government almost never relinquishes powers it has once gained. He was willing to live in a more volatile, more dangerous, more chaotic world if he could remain free rather than to seek security and order at the cost of his independence and the panoply of his freedoms. The Jeffersonian must insist that any security measure be candidly explained to the American people, that it be robustly debated, that it be subject to the most unrelenting court review, that dissent be cherished, that any such measure be temporary, and that the government that undertakes it exhibit profound reluctance rather than zeal and satisfaction in the face of such increased authority.

The twenty-first century opens with unprecedented anxiety about the future of the Enlightenment's legacy of freedom. The cheapening and democratization of violence and terror have led millions of otherwise rational people to want their governments to do whatever it will take to provide for their basic security and standard of living. Such people would prefer not to relinquish any of their freedoms—just the opposite—but given the choice between maintenance of their access to security and the fruits of life, on the one hand, and the enjoyment of the full complement of their liberties in a rather more dangerous world, on the other, they quietly vote for their material rather than their spiritual well-being.

The plain truth is that it is not at all clear that the principles of the Enlightenment can survive in a world where the technologies of terror are more widely and inexpensively accessible than at any previous time in human history, and when one act of spasmodic violence can shatter the lives not merely of a handful of citizens, but of hundreds of thousands or millions of people. The twenty-first century will call the bluff of the principles of the Enlightenment in ways that would astonish Voltaire, Condorcet, Rousseau, or Thomas Jefferson. All those universalist statements about human aspiration voiced by the great minds of the eighteenth century may turn out to have been contingent on a certain technological, demographic, and geographic moment in human history. That would be a tragedy for western civilization, but it cannot be ruled out.

Even so, the Jeffersonians will not succumb to pessimism and they will resist loudly—but with unclouded eyes—the siren song of security, order, and the status quo.

Optimism

The plan of reading which I have formed [for my daughter Martha] is considerably different from that which I think would be most proper for her sex in any other country than America. I am obliged to extend my views beyond herself, and consider her as the head of a little family of her own. The chance that in marriage she will draw a blockhead I calculate at about fourteen to one, and course that the education of her family will probably rest on her own ideas and directions without assistance.

Jefferson to Francois de Barbe-Marbois
December 5, 1783

Optimism

A JEFFERSONIAN is a willful optimist. At a low moment, Jefferson wrote, "I was born to lose everything I love." Four of his six white children died in their infancy. A fifth, his younger daughter Maria (Polly) died in 1804 at the age of 25. Jefferson's father, mother, favorite sister Jane, and closest friend Dabney Carr, all died prematurely by twenty-first century standards.

Jefferson lived in serious debt through most of his adult life, and by 1815, the debt was so massive that he was barely able to maintain enough solvency to live out his life at Monticello. This was a source—occasionally—of great stress in Jefferson's life. At any given moment after his second term as president, Jefferson was in a position to realize that his lifestyle was economically insupportable, and that if he actually lived within his means, he would be forced to sell off almost everything he owned, including perhaps Monticello, and that he would need to forego many of his most cherished habits of accumulation and consumption: fine imported wines, books, music and musical instruments, furnishings and finishing hardware for his building projects, house wares, works of art, and much more.

Jefferson knew that his ownership of slaves, his need to buy and sell slaves, hunt them down when they ran away, have them whipped for insubordination, and evade pointed questions put to him by his Enlightenment friends about his dependency on an institution they all agreed was morally and legally repugnant, was a blot upon his reputation as an advocate for human rights. He must have known that the judgment of history was bound to catch up with him, and condemn him for violating the very codes for which he was the foremost articulator of his time, and perhaps for all time.

Jefferson spoke frequently of the joys and harmony of his family life, but behind the agreeable rhetoric lay a highly dysfunctional family. Jefferson's daughter Martha's husband, Thomas Mann Randolph, had a flash temper, and he was subject to nervous fits and periods of alienation from home, family, and community. Jefferson's sons-in-law (particularly the mercurial Randolph) were engaged in a struggle for the affection and respect of their father-in-law, and both daughters strained to keep their father central to their lives and hearts (as he wished it) without making it impossible for them to bond fully with their husbands. The specter of debt and decay hung over Monticello from 1809 onward. Jefferson's granddaughter Ann married an abusive man who beat her and, as a consequence, became involved in a public brawl with Jefferson's grandson Thomas Jefferson Randolph in downtown Charlottesville. Jefferson's daughter Martha's sister-in-law was involved in a notorious adulterous liaison which ended in alleged infanticide and a spectacular public trial. It was not, in short, all Palladian neoclassicism in Albemarle County, Virginia, whatever Jefferson might say in his voluminous correspondence. Jefferson's Virginia was in many respects closer to *Gone with the Wind* than Horatian Arcadia.

And yet, Jefferson somehow remained optimistic right up to the end.

Some of Jefferson's optimism was temperamental, but more was the result of a deliberate choice. His private *Decalogue* (1825) indicates how important will was in his pursuit of happiness.

1. Never put off till to-morrow what you can do to-day.

2. Never trouble another for what you can do yourself.

7. Nothing is troublesome that we do willingly.

8. How much pain have cost us the evils which have never happened.

9. Take things always by their smooth handle.[9]

Like Franklin and Washington, Jefferson set out early in life to discipline his soul and rub off the rough edges from his character. He believed in self-mastery. He believed that a person of self-restraint could avoid the spasms of irrational behavior that bring chaos and suffering to life. Avoidance of crisis brought peace and harmony to one's existence, and a sustained period of harmony led one to be optimistic about the prospects of life. In other words, some part of Jeffersonian optimism was the result of leading a life of rational calculation, rather than impulse. It also involved a commitment to social harmony.

In a letter to his favorite grandson Thomas Jefferson Randolph, Jefferson recommended that the boy adopt "artificial good humor."

In truth, politeness is artificial good humor, it covers the natural want of it, and ends by rendering habitual a substitute nearly equivalent to the real virtue. It is the practice of sacrificing to those whom we meet in society, all the little conveniences and preferences which will gratify them, and deprive us of "nothing worth a moment's consideration; it is the giving a pleasing and flattering turn to our expressions, which

9. To Thomas Jefferson Smith, February 21, 1825.

will conciliate others, and make them pleased with us as well as themselves. How cheap a price for the good will of another!"[10]

Jefferson appears to have passed through eighty-three years without often (perhaps ever) lapsing himself into rudeness and aggression. He was essentially a character out of a Jane Austen novel: civil, graceful, polite, reasonable, euphemistic, and poised. He subscribed to some variation of the golden rule: He who treats others with civility and generosity will usually be treated well in return, and the result of this tacit quid pro quo is that there are fewer blows to one's cheerful view of life.

Perhaps Jefferson adopted "artificial optimism" in the face of all the losses and setbacks of his life. One senses that below the serene Palladian surface of Jefferson's persona was a more volatile, at times volcanic, being, and that Jefferson set out—at some early point in his life—to achieve stoic imperturbability in order to avoid letting his emotions run away with his peace of mind. Late in life Jefferson lamented to John Adams that he had known almost unbearable losses. "There are, I acknolege [sic], even in the happiest life, some terrible convulsions, heavy set-offs against the opposite page of the account," he admitted, but almost immediately he returned to his willful optimism. "I think with you that it is a good world, on the whole; that it has been framed on a principle of benevolence, and more pleasure than pain dealt out to us. There are, indeed (who might say nay), gloomy and hypochondriac minds, inhabitants of diseased bodies, disgusted with the present and despairing of the future, always counting that the worst will happen because it may happen."[11]

10. To Thomas Jefferson Randolph, November 24, 1808.
11. To John Adams, April 8, 1816.

Whatever the cause, it is indisputable that Jefferson spent virtually no time indulging in negativity.

It was entirely rational that an Enlightenment philosopher like Jefferson looked upon the future with optimism. As he put it in his First Inaugural Address, the United States possessed "a chosen country, with room enough for our descendants to the thousandth and thousandth generation." He believed that the Atlantic Ocean was a three-thousand-mile moat that separated the pastoral innocence of America from the madness, havoc, and the dark history of the Old World. He was nearly in solidarity with Thomas Paine when the great pamphleteer proclaimed that "we have it in our power to begin the world over again." Surely Jefferson believed that he was living in the best of all possible times, in what would soon become the best of all republics in the best of all possible worlds—worlds providentially designed by a benign Newtonian God. The North American continent, meanwhile, was from a white European point of view both a tabula rasa upon which the Americans were destined to write their utopia, and the most stupendous treasury of untapped resources on earth. No nation, Jefferson believed, had ever begun its rendezvous with destiny with so many incontestable advantages. In Jefferson's mind, any American who could see all this and remain a pessimist was fit only for Bedlam. When former President George H. W. Bush used to respond to doubt by effusing, "We're America!" he was articulating the Jeffersonian optimism.

The only note of shadow in this American Arcadia came, appropriately, from the deepening crisis over slavery. To John Holmes, he wrote on April 22, 1802, "I regret that I am now to die in the belief, that the useless sacrifice of themselves by the generation of 1776, to acquire self-government and happiness to their country, is to be thrown away by the unwise and unworthy passions of their sons, and that my only consolation is to be, that I live not to weep over it."[12]

In the face of the madness and the destructiveness of the twentieth century, Jefferson's belief in the essential "goodness of man" seems fatuous, perhaps even obscene. Between Freud and Hitler and Pol Pot and Hiroshima, the Enlightenment's rosy picture of human nature and the human project was dealt fundamental and perhaps fatal blows. If Jefferson could believe that all rational beings see the benevolence of things, a similarly confident social observer today might argue that all rational beings must be disenchanted realists—believers that humankind is born to botch the world.

The appropriate Jeffersonian response at the beginning of the twenty-first century would seem to be an Augustinian diagnosis and a sober Jeffersonianism in prescription. In other words, today's Jeffersonians ought to acknowledge that human nature—if human behavior is a fair measure—is an open indictment of the Enlightenment's optimism, and yet there is good reason to believe that under the right circumstances (see education) the world can be made better and better and the roughnesses of human response can be gradually worn off, that most (perhaps all) governments will come to be republics that reflect and embrace the sovereignty and the will of the people, and that the rights tradition, born on the fourth of July, will continue to destabilize despotic regimes all over the earth.

Jefferson has been called a "grieving optimist" because many of the people he most loved died before

12. To John Holmes, April 22, 1820.

his eyes, some of them at unbearably young ages. Perhaps it might be said that the Jeffersonians of the twenty-first century must necessarily be "grieving optimists," because they still believe in the dream of America, the perfectibility of life, and the possibilities of rationality and the leavening power of education, in spite of the cataclysms of the centuries following the high water mark of the Enlightenment.

To be a Jeffersonian is to be an optimist in spite of the facts. To be a Jeffersonian is to be intoxicated by the very idea of America.

Freedom of Thought

The error seems not sufficiently eradicated, that the operations of the mind, as well as the acts of the body, are subject to the coercion of the laws. But our rulers can have no authority over such natural rights, only as we have submitted to them. The rights of conscience we never submitted, we could not submit. We are answerable for them to our God. The legitimate powers of government extend to such acts only as are injurious to others. But it does me no injury for my neighbor to say there are twenty gods, or no God. It neither picks my pocket nor breaks my leg. If it be said, his testimony in a court of justice cannot be relied on, reject it then, and be the stigma on him. Constraint may make him worse. by making him a hypocrite, but it will never make him a truer man. It may fix him obstinately in his errors, but will not cure them. Reason and free inquiry are the only effectual agents against error. Give a loose to them, they will support the true religion by bringing every false one to their tribunal, to the test of their investigation. They are the natural enemies of error, and of error only.

Jefferson, *Virginia Statute for Religious Freedom*

Freedom of Thought

A JEFFERSONIAN believes in unlimited freedom of thought. The central principle of the Enlightenment was that no idea had special status, no idea need be protected from scrutiny. The Enlightenment argued for a free marketplace of ideas, where all ideas would be permitted to compete for the hearts and minds of the public without the slightest censorship. In the preamble to his Virginia Statute for Religious Liberty, Jefferson argued that the only ideas that required government support were suspect ones. Jefferson envisioned a nation of robust discourse, with a cheerful commitment to dissent.

As the twenty-first century begins, Americans have a paradoxical relationship with free thought and free speech. On the one hand, we have more incidental freedom than any people who have ever lived. We can travel at will throughout the United States, and slip into the profoundest anonymity in almost any locality, publish or purchase obnoxious, irresponsible, pornographic, bigoted, racist, murderous, and seditious tracts, and shout publicly that the president or the chief justice of the Supreme Court or the bishop of the Catholic Church is a thief, warmonger, swine, imbecile, pederast, or foreign agent—all this with perfect impunity. We can purchase virtually anything anywhere on credit, and our associations are almost never regulated in any way. We can consume as many of the earth's resources as we can afford to pay for. We can profess any religious sensibility, from the dourest Presbyterianism to the most sensualist New Age massage cultism, from radical double predestination to Wicca Eroticism—all without the slightest governmental interference—and with tax exemption to boot. By the standards of the Age of Jefferson, we are breathtakingly free, freer than any people who ever walked the earth.

On the other hand, as all foreign visitors (beginning with Alexis de Tocqueville) realize, there is a numbing homogeneity to American thought. Left entirely free to think for ourselves, we have permitted our capitalist systems of dissemination to press our free minds into severely limited channels. In fact, we invite it. We are free, but we freely watch the same television programs, buy the same products because of the obscene illusion—now universal in our advertising—that our soul's restlessness can be assuaged by the purchase of Brand X. We have voluntarily enslaved ourselves to the jejune, the superficial, and the faddish. Americans are free but they are not intellectually mature or culturally sophisticated. Perhaps it is fear of the vast outback of our intellectual freedom that impels us to cluster together in a handful of cultural clearings, and to volunteer to be sheeplike even though there is no determined shepherd in our midst. The good Jeffersonian is always disappointed to find that her or his mind is gravitating to conventional wisdom and faddish notions.

The twenty-first century will present us with the greatest (perhaps final) test of the ideals of the Enlightenment. The electronic revolution will soon bring about a discourse infrastructure in which anyone can post any idea in public space at any time, without peer review, or the cumbersomeness and expense of the disseminating technologies of the past. A breathtaking chaos of ideas will take their place on the stage of twenty-first century life, and no institution, public or private, will be able to police that stage to limit or forbid the worst excesses of free expression: sedition, corrosive cynicism, character assassination, disclosure of industrial secrets, disclosure of weapons design, theft of intellectual property (which will come to be seen as a quaint notion from the past), pornography, hate speech, unrestrained dogmatics, or exploitation of the powerless.

In a sense the new world of the electronic revolution will call the bluff of the ideals of the Enlightenment and make us ask ourselves if we really desire a "free marketplace of ideas." Given the abuses that are guaranteed to characterize this new order of the ages (novus ordo seclorum), the temptation will be to back away from the libertarian model of discourse and establish some form of thought policing. This the Jefferson must resist, however difficult that conviction makes her or his life. We are going to have to get serious about education and the humanities if we do not wish to be that thing that Jefferson most feared, "a nation ignorant and [temporarily] free."

Believing with you that religion is a matter which lies solely between man and his God, that he owes account to none other for his faith or his worship, that the legislative powers of government reach actions only, and not opinions, I contemplate with sovereign reverence that act of the whole American people which declared that their legislature should "make no law respecting an establishment of religion, or prohibiting the free exercise thereof," thus building a wall of separation between Church and State. Adhering to this expression of the supreme will of the nation in behalf of the rights of conscience, I shall see with sincere satisfaction the progress of those sentiments which tend to restore to man all his natural rights, convinced he has no natural right in opposition to his social duties.

Jefferson to the Danbury Baptists
January 1, 1802

Church and State

A JEFFERSONIAN is firmly committed to the "wall of separation between church and state." However much it may annoy conservatives and evangelicals, the Jeffersonian gently but firmly insists that there is no place in the public square for crosses, prayer, nativity scenes, the ten commandments, the pledge of allegiance (offensive to a Jeffersonian on other grounds, as well), or any other paeans to the Judeo-Christian tradition or any other religious system. A Jeffersonian resists—with historical evidence—the silly notion that the Founding Fathers intended a Christian commonwealth. To be sure, most of the Founding Fathers were Christians, and many of them believed that God's providence shone in some special way on the American experiment, but most of them understood that the government of the United States needed to be punctiliously neutral on questions of conscience and religion, that a citizen's religious sensibilities were entirely private, and that any governmental endorsement of religious activity, even ecumenical religious activity, was a quasi-establishment of an official religion, and therefore impermissible in a free society.

In spite of all that the evangelicals pretend, the Constitution of the United States is entirely silent on questions of religion. God is never mentioned in the Constitution, not even as the "Creator" or "Nature's God" (both from the Declaration of Independence). A Jeffersonian believes that the judiciary rightly interprets the meaning of the First Amendment as prohibiting virtually all overt religious expression in the public arena, and denies the notion that the judicial decisions of the second half of the twentieth century deliberately misread the Constitution to promote a secularist agenda that the Founding Fathers would have found abhorrent.

A Jeffersonian believes that if the evangelicals don't like the increasing enforcement of the secularist intent of the Founding Fathers, they should create a movement to amend the Constitution or tear it up altogether. Short of that, they should go about their private (and absolutely unmolested!) worship in private spaces (chapels, synagogues, churches, private schools, summer camps), and show more respect for the social compact.

Jeffersonians are freethinkers, skeptics, and rationalists, which means that if they are Christians they are nominal and habitual Christians rather than believers in the divinity of Jesus. Jefferson believed that Jesus was one of the greatest men who ever lived, certainly the greatest ethicist, and that a simple adherence to the ethical code of Jesus would bring about paradise on earth; but that the metaphysics of Christianity—from the miracles to the apocalypse, from original sin to the Trinity or the efficacy of prayer—were inherited mythologies that embarrass the validity of Jesus' message, and which can (and should) be discarded by beings worthy of the title "rational."

Even so, Jefferson respected the religious sensibilities of all unself-righteous others, and defended to the death their right to worship any god they pleased, so long as they did not try to prescribe religious activity for others.

The Jeffersonian is a one-person ACLU, politely but firmly insisting upon the utter neutrality of the state with respect to questions of conscience.

Friendship

The friendship which has subsisted between us, now half a century, and the harmony of our political principles and pursuits, have been sources of constant happiness to me through that long period. And if I remove beyond the reach of attentions to the University, or beyond the bourne of life itself, as I soon must, it is a comfort to leave that institution under your care, and an assurance that it will not be wanting. It has also been a great solace to me, to believe that you are engaged in vindicating to posterity the course we have pursued for preserving to them, in all their purity, the blessings of self-government, which we had assisted too in acquiring for them. If ever the earth has beheld a system of administration conducted with a single and steadfast eye to the general interest and happiness of those committed to it, one which, protected by truth, can never know reproach, it is that to which our lives have been devoted. To myself you have been a pillar of support through life. Take care of me when dead, and be assured that I shall leave with you my last affections.

Jefferson to James Madison, February 17, 1826

I had rather be shut up in a very modest cottage, with my books, my family and a few old friends, dining on simple bacon, and letting the world roll on as it liked than to occupy the most splendid post which any human power can give.

Jefferson to Alexander Donald, February 7, 1788

Friendship

A JEFFERSONIAN is an excellent friend. Thomas Jefferson had a gigantic capacity for friendship. He saw the world through the twin lenses of large Enlightenment abstractions ("all men are created equal") and harmonious friendship. He had a gift for placing himself in the mindset of his friends, understanding their sensibilities, sympathizing with the complexities of their lives, and anticipating their wants. He wrote to his friends often, generously, and with a profound respect for their souls. He was intensely loyal. In many respects, he understood that friendship is the highest form of human relationship—voluntary, based on affinity and shared values, and uncluttered by the dense emotions and dysfunctions of family life. Jefferson's closest adult friend was James Madison, but a list of his friends would occupy many pages of text. Among them were James Monroe, John Adams, Abigail Adams, Thomas Paine, Maria Cosway, Benjamin Franklin, George Washington, John Page, Dabney Carr, John Taylor, Benjamin Rush, David Rittenhouse, Joseph Priestley, Lafayette, and Benjamin Smith Barton. Somehow Jefferson had the talent of making each of his friends feel especially important, loved, and central to his happiness.

Jeffersonians love friendship and pay special attention to its many satisfactions. They try to give their best energies to their friends, and they spend time devising ways to find perfect gifts for them, serve their interests, listen to their concerns, and resonate fully with their souls. They measure the world according to the friendships they form, and they seek friendship not for what it can do for their careers or their public lives, but for what it can do for their private pursuit of happiness.

Friendship is, in the long run, a great deal of work, and it requires a steadiness that is really at odds with one's sense of autonomy and productivity. But Jeffersonians find a way to make the many claims of friendship seem lovely and un-burdensome.

The Process of National Renewal

They were written [notes on the corruption of British judges] at a time of life when I was bold in the pursuit of knowledge, never fearing to follow truth and reason to whatever results they led, and bearding every authority which stood in their way. This must be the apology, if you find the conclusions bolder than historical facts and principles will warrant.

Jefferson to Thomas Cooper
February 10, 1814

The Process of National Renewal

A JEFFERSONIAN believes that a great people must reconstitute, redefine, refashion, and rethink itself from time to time, at least once per generation. In a famous letter to James Madison, Jefferson suggested that the American people tear up their constitution every nineteen or so years. Madison was, to say the least, not convinced, but that did not deter Jefferson, who advocated a literalist adherence to the principle of the consent of the governed. The "earth belongs to the living," Jefferson wrote, meaning that the systems, constitutions, institutions, and protocols of one generation are not automatically appropriate for the next one, and that even where they are appropriate, the unborn ought not to be imposed on by those who have passed from the scene.

The more cautious Madison replied that continuity, order, and human reverence for tradition are too valuable to jeopardize, even assuming Jefferson was right about the absolute rights of the majority of the living generation. Madison found order comforting, while Jefferson realized that it can be a claustrophobic, even a quietly despotic, force in human affairs.

Jefferson was not afraid of change, and he did not believe that the way things happen to be is necessarily the way they ought to be. More importantly, he did not believe things were as they were because they had developed in an inevitable way. He understood that, natural rights aside, most social structures are in fact artificial constructs that bear no special resonance to nature or the fundamentals of existence. "We might as well require a man to wear still the coat which fitted him when a boy, as civilized society to remain ever under the regimen of their barbarous ancestors,"[13] Jefferson wrote to Samuel Kercheval in 1816.

Jefferson believed that some issues are so fundamental that they cannot be resolved by routine legislation. This is particularly the case when reforms are requested from holders of power who might stand to lose from a change in the status quo (term limits, redistricting). Jefferson understood that this is the great advantage of the revolutionary moment. When the civilization has broken down and people have returned to a state of nature, they have it in their power to refashion the world without having to struggle against the massive inertia of existing institutions. Things that exhibit hidebound tenacity within the existing order and seem too deeply rooted to be altered, turn out to collapse without great drama once their artificial aura of legitimacy has been shattered. From time to time a culture needs to return to a state of nature, to the true anarchic sovereignty of the people, so that the people can reconstitute themselves without unnecessary influence from what Hamilton called "the wise, the rich, and the wellborn."

Jefferson's unstated motto was that there is nothing magical in the way things are. He believed that he stood at the dawn of a new era in which every institution, every habit, every system, every cultural code, every belief, and every received truth would be examined according to the dictates of reason and good sense, and its capacity to promote human dignity and happiness.

13. To Samuel Kercheval, July 12, 1816.

The Pursuit of Happiness

I am savage enough to prefer the woods, the wilds, and the independence of Monticello to all the brilliant pleasures of this gay capital. I shall, therefore, rejoin myself to my native country with new attachments and with exaggerated esteem for its advantages; for though there is less wealth there, there is more freedom, more ease, and less misery. I am as happy nowhere else, and in no other society, and all my wishes end, where I hope my days will end, at Monticello. Too many scenes of happiness mingle themselves with all the recollections of my native woods and fields to suffer them to be supplanted in my affection by any other.

Jefferson to Baron de Geismar, September 6, 1785 and to George Gilmer, August 11, 1787

The Pursuit of Happiness

A JEFFERSONIAN believes in the good life. Jefferson considered himself an Epicurean, though in the severely virtuous rather than hedonistic sense of the term. He surrounded himself with beauty: in architecture, in his gardens and fields, in his books and furnishings, in art and in music. There was, in Iago's words, "a daily beauty in his life" that ought to inspire us to live with something like equal dignity and happiness.

Monticello is a world of rich textures, excellent sight lines, beautiful vistas, symmetrical design motifs, and lovely accoutrements. Jefferson was incapable of living with the mediocre, the imprecise, or the jejune. He brought an exquisite sensibility to all that he ever did. In a sense it is a pity that he lived part of his life in the political arena, because there—least of all—could he shape the contours of his world into sweet harmony. He lamented that politics is a crude, aggressive, and messy business, and he infinitely preferred to live his life in a world of decanters, books, cabinets, and scientific instruments.

Jefferson believed that we exist to be happy, not to struggle through life or perform duties or deny ourselves pleasures. There is nothing dour or Calvinist in the Jeffersonian temperament. No day should unfold without the pleasures of food, wine, nature, flowers, family, friendship, books, art, music, and contemplation. And love.

His motto was, "Take things always by their smooth handle."

Jefferson was a thoroughgoing rationalist, who believed that one of the keys to happiness was the avoidance of conflict and pain. "Do not bite at the bait of pleasure till you know there is no hook beneath it," he wrote in his famous love letter to Maria Cosway (1786), "My Head and My Heart." "The art of life is the art of avoiding pain: and he is the best pilot who steers clearest of the rocks and shoals with which it is beset....The most effectual means of being secure against pain is to retire within ourselves, and to suffice for our own happiness." This was the stoic strain in Jefferson's character, born of a classical education and early and profound experience of pain and loss.

The Jeffersonian has a highly evolved aesthetic sense. To enter his or her world is to understand that the accoutrements of life are a measure of the quality of one's soul, and that it is the duty of mature human beings to surround themselves with objects and structures that declare to the world what is really valuable—and lovely. One need only examine a single Jefferson document—choose one at random—to see the exquisiteness of his penmanship and the delicacy of his temperament. His letters are works of art in both senses: they show an immense epistolary artistry, and they are beautiful to look at irrespective of the meaning of the words they present to the world.

Jeffersonians prefer the art of living to power, success, wealth, or status.

SIR,-Your favor of the 15th of June is received, and I am very thankful for the kindness of its expressions respecting myself. But it ascribes to me merits which I do not claim. I was only of a band devoted to the cause of independence, all of whom exerted equally their best endeavors for its success, and have a common right to the merits of its acquisition. So also is the civil revolution of 1801. Very many and very meritorious were the worthy patriots who assisted in bringing back our government to its republican tack. To preserve it in that, will require unremitting vigilance.

Jefferson to William Barry
July 2, 1822

Meritocracy

A JEFFERSONIAN believes that a great nation champions merit rather than privilege. Jefferson called those who enjoy arbitrary success in life the "pseudo-aristocrats," and he urged the United States to legislate impediments to their ascendancy, or at the very least not prop up their privilege. As much as possible, Jefferson wanted to eliminate artificial and socially privileged distinctions between individuals and to create a level playing field on which anybody could achieve excellence if she or he showed sufficient industry. To John Adams he wrote, "May we not even say, that that form of government is the best, which provides the most effectually for a pure selection of these natural aristoi into the offices of government? The artificial aristocracy is a mischievous ingredient in government, and provision should be made to prevent its ascendancy."[14]

Jefferson knew that in any society an artificial order will emerge in which certain individuals and families will attain a prominence that has little or nothing to do with merit. Social conservatives will then come to argue that the way things are is the way things ought to be. Their view was revealingly articulated a century later by coal mine operator George Baer, an executive with the Philadelphia & Reading Railroad, who responded to labor unrest by declaring, "The rights and interests of the laboring man will be protected and cared for—not by the labor agitators, but by the Christian men to whom God in His infinite wisdom has given control of the property interests of the country."

Jefferson understood that the powerful and privileged will always take care of themselves, that they

14. To John Adams, October 28, 1813.

need no help from the state. Indeed, the danger is that they will become the state. He believed that genuine merit is evenly distributed across the population base and that the state has a vital interest in nurturing merit outside the halls of privilege.

Jeffersonians never believe that they are entitled to the privileges which they nevertheless make the best use of in the interests of the commonwealth. Whether they are aristocrats by birth (what he dismissed as "pseudo-aristocrats") or privileged thanks to hard work and integrity (what he called "natural aristocrats"), they labor every day to earn again their status at the apex of American life.

Wine

I rejoice, as a moralist, at the prospect of a reduction of the duties on wine by our national Legislature. It is an error to view a tax on that liquor as merely a tax on the rich. It is a prohibition of its use to the middling class of our citizens, and a condemnation of them to the poison of whisky, which is desolating their houses. No nation is drunken where wine is cheap; and none sober, where the dreariness of wine substitutes ardent spirits as the common beverage. It is, in truth, the only antidote to the bane of whisky.

Jefferson to M. de Neuville, 1818

Wine

A JEFFERSONIAN cannot live without wine. A Jeffersonian cannot live without music. A Jeffersonian cannot live without books. A Jeffersonian cannot live without friendship. A Jeffersonian cannot live without food fresh from the garden. A Jeffersonian cannot live without love.

The Perfectability of Life

I am for encouraging the progress of science in all its branches; and not for raising a hue and cry against the sacred name of philosophy; for awing the human mind by stories of raw-head and bloody bones to a distrust of its own vision; and to repose implicitly on that of others; to go backwards instead of forwards, to look for improvement; to believe that government, religion, morality, and every other science were in the highest perfection in ages of the darkest ignorance, and that nothing can ever be devised more perfect than what was established by our forefathers.

Jefferson to Elbridge Gerry
January 26, 1799

The Perfectibility of Life

A JEFFERSONIAN believes that the world can be made better, that every device, habit, institution, and system is capable of being redesigned to perform its function more efficiently or more delightfully, and that we must never accept inefficiency, unfairness, or corruption merely because things have always been done that way. Jefferson believed that the past was mostly a collection of mistakes, and that the traditions of a culture did not deserve any respect beyond their measurable merit. Jefferson believed that we should be prepared to sweep away imperfect systems and try something more rational or more just, and that hoary tradition was no justification to continue any habit of culture. Jefferson further believed that we should shake things up from time to time, merely to remind ourselves that nothing is inherently entitled to permanence. He was aware that such a philosophy will sometimes create chaos—but it did not seem to bother him much.

In the Declaration of Independence, Jefferson agreed that systems should not be revolutionized "for light and transient causes," but his general outlook was that rational beings could and should tinker boldly with the world about them, that there was nothing sacrosanct except natural right, and that as long as reformers remembered that their duty was to improve the world for the benefit of all mankind, they should not be unduly constrained by the dead hand of the past.

When Jefferson saw an inefficient plow in the course of his European travels, he sat down immediately to design an improved plowshare, the "moldboard of least resistance." He was not afraid to reform America's coinage, her land survey and tenure systems, the metric system, Senate parliamentary procedures, the workings of John Hawkins' polygraph, the university curriculum, or existing library classification systems.

A Jeffersonian believes that most of the softwares of the world are artificial constructions, not infallible echoes of the natural structure of life, and that they should be cheerfully discarded the moment a more rational, more efficient, more just, or more practical system can be devised or discerned. Jeffersonians are rational busybodies who are always asking, "Can it be improved, for whose benefit, and at what cost?"

The Active Life

Walking is the best possible exercise. Habituate yourself to walk very far. The Europeans value themselves on having subdued the horse to the uses of man; but I doubt whether we have not lost more than we have gained by the use of this animal.

Jefferson to Peter Carr
August 19, 1785

The Active Life

A JEFFERSONIAN is indefatigably active. Jefferson prided himself on never wasting a single moment. He believed that idleness is the parent of ennui, melancholia, depression, error, self-indulgence, and what his Christian colleagues called sin. To his daughter Martha, he wrote, "Determine never to be idle. No person will have occasion to complain of the want of time who never loses any. It is wonderful how much may be done if we are always doing."[15] The idea of "kicking back," vacationing on the beach at Cabo, spending an evening eating and drinking in a tavern, or attending a football game (much less a tailgate party!) holds no appeal for Jefferson, who believed that the world is so utterly fascinating that only a fool would succumb to idleness when she or he could be reading, writing, growing, or designing something instead. Jefferson believed that unrelenting activity was a source of energy for still more unrelenting activity.

Jefferson's idea of relaxation was a long walk in nature or a horseback ride, or a swath of time spent puttering in the garden in the cool of the evening.

Jefferson was something of an efficiency expert and he took pleasure in constructing grids of how his own time might be made better use of. He never ducked an opportunity to lay out a course of reading—and of life discipline—for his friends and protégés. How he would have thrilled to the organizational tools of our time, the personal digital assistants, the clocking and monitoring devices, the technological efficiencies of our communications devices. One need merely imagine Jefferson with a laptop computer to feel his ecstasy. He made the most of the low-tech tools of his own

15. To Martha Jefferson Marseilles, May 5, 1787.

time. Imagine what he would have done with ours. Imagine how much he would fret over our inefficient and narcissistic use of our magnificent tools.

Americans frequently ask how much a man of such enormous accomplishment could have slept. The answer is that Jefferson slept more than most geniuses because he believed in the importance of the life of good sense and moderation. There is nothing of the tortured artist in Jefferson's character. Jefferson's view was that it doesn't really matter how many hours one sleeps at night. What matters is what one does with her or his waking hours.

A Little Rebellion Now and Then

It can never be too often repeated, that the time for fixing every essential right on a legal basis is while our rulers are honest, and ourselves united. From the conclusion of this war we shall be going down hill. It will not then be necessary to resort every moment to the people for support. They will be forgotten, therefore, and their rights disregarded. They will forget themselves, but in the sole faculty of making money, and will never think of uniting to effect a due respect for their rights. The shackles, therefore, which shall not be knocked off at the conclusion of this war, will remain on us long, will be made heavier and heavier, till our rights shall revive or expire in a convulsion.

Jefferson, *Notes on the State of Virginia*

A Little Rebellion Now and Then

A JEFFERSONIAN believes in rebellion, as peaceful as possible, and as bloody as necessary. In other words, a Jeffersonian is aware that some problems never get solved through routine legislation. Throughout his lifetime Jefferson shocked his contemporaries by his statements endorsing armed rebellion, defending the validity of the French Revolution, including the Terror, and his general belief that societies need to be rocked by rebellion now and then to keep them from forgetting to serve the rights and happiness of humankind.

Jefferson never struck another human being in the whole course of his life. He was a harmony obsessive who shrank from controversy and everything sordid, rough, and uncivil in life. In other words, he was not a man of violence, and he invariably preferred the smooth path rather than confrontation or struggle. But he knew that terror is an essential tool in the quest for human liberty, and he rightly predicted that "rivers of blood may yet flow between them [the tyrannized peoples of the earth] and their object."[16]

Jeffersonians, like their master, are men and women profoundly committed to peace and harmony, and they are not fond of bloodshed in any of its forms, but they are careful not to condemn acts of terror out of hand. They keep in mind two things: first, that most terrorists do not delight in mayhem, but turn to it only as the "last melancholy resort" after all peaceful and "legitimate" attempts to call attention to injustice have been exhausted; second, that terror works, that it has the capacity to call the world's attention to issues that would otherwise be ignored ad infinitum.

16. To John Adams, January 11, 1816.

For Jeffersonians, the greatest crime against happiness is learning to live with corruption, institutional indifference, and injustice merely because one is afraid to "take arms against a sea of troubles and by opposing end them." Those who renounce the use of violence in advance condemn themselves to degradation and enslavement, because established powers are unwilling to commit themselves to the same code of engagement, and they count upon the general peacefulness and passivity of their populations in order to dominate them.

Your situation, thrown at such a distance from us, & alone, cannot but give us all great anxieties for you. As much has been secured for you, by your particular position and the acquaintance to which you have been recommended, as could be done towards shielding you from the dangers which surround you. But thrown on a wide world, among entire strangers, without a friend or guardian to advise, so young too and with so little experience of mankind, your dangers are great, & still your safety must rest on yourself. A determination never to do what is wrong, prudence and good humor, will go far towards securing to you the estimation of the world. When I recollect that at 14 years of age, the whole care & direction of myself was thrown on myself entirely, without a relation or friend qualified to advise or guide me, and recollect the various sorts of bad company with which I associated from time to time, I am astonished I did not turn off with some of them, & become worthless to society as they were. I had the good fortune to become acquainted very early with some characters of very high standing, and to feel the incessant wish that I could ever become what they were. Under temptations & difficulties, I would ask myself what would Dr. Small, Mr. Wythe, Peyton Randolph do in this situation? What course in it will insure me their approbation? I am certain that this mode of deciding on my conduct, tended more to its correctness than any reasoning powers I possessed. Knowing the even & dignified line they pursued, I could never doubt for a moment which of two courses would be in character for them.

Jefferson to Thomas Jefferson Randolph,
November 24, 1808

Mentoring

A JEFFERSONIAN is a mentor. Jefferson benefited from gifted mentors, and he became a collector of protégés himself. Jefferson's father Peter died when he was just fourteen years old. That left a hole in Jefferson's life that was never completely filled. Jefferson was fortunate that as a young man he won the affection and respect of two great mentors: William Small, professor of mathematics at the College of William and Mary; and George Wythe, the self-taught Greek and legal scholar, who practiced law in Williamsburg. Later Jefferson said Small "set the destinies of my life," by putting good books in front of him and urging him to be a genuine freethinker. Jefferson could never praise Wythe sufficiently for his commitment to classical learning and a deep rooting in the humanities.

Jefferson served as mentor to a significant number of individuals, most notably James Monroe, Meriwether Lewis, William Small, his nephew Peter Carr, and his grandson Thomas Jefferson Randolph. Jefferson saw his role as providing reading lists for gifted young men, pressing them to master languages and to read deeply and widely, and to provide some guidance about moral development. Jefferson can be said to have politically mentored James Madison (who hardly needed a mentor) and James Monroe, who served in the presidency after Jefferson retired. By mentoring these two remarkable individuals, Jefferson in a sense obtained for himself a third, fourth, fifth, and sixth term as president. Madison and Monroe served their mentor in part by continuing to carry out his principles when they followed him into the presidency.

Though Jefferson would not have put it quite this way, mentors have an advantage over one's parents because they are more disinterested, more emotionally detached, more purely generous.

Jeffersonians take the time to become mentors because they understand that adolescence is a perilous time in which promising young people need the help of gifted older people who wish to see them blossom into genius. They know that in many respects the world is repaired one person at a time, and that by shaping the development of one remarkable person, a mentor may in the end be shaping the development of an institution, a community, perhaps even a culture. Jeffersonians become mentors because they remember their own development, and feel deep appreciation for those who intervened at precisely the right moment to take them to a higher level of achievement and understanding.

Almost every extraordinary achiever can point to a mentor who made all the difference. That was certainly true of Jefferson and William Small. Although mentoring has fallen somewhat into disfavor in our time (thanks to our hypersensitivity about intimacy between older and younger people), Jeffersonians carefully persevere, knowing that the mentor–apprentice relationship is not only one of the most important, but also one of the most precious and satisfying, relationships we can have.

The Primacy of Science

What a field we have at our doors to signalize our-selves in! The botany of America is far from being exhausted, its mineralogy is untouched, and its natural history or zoology totally mistaken and mis-represented. . . . It is the work to which the young men whom you are forming [at Harvard] should lay their hands. We have spent the prime of our lives in procuring them the precious blessings of liberty. Let them spend theirs in showing that it is the great parent of science and of virtue; and that a nation will be great in both always in proportion as it is free.

Jefferson to Dr. Joseph Willard
March 24, 1789

The Primacy of Science

A JEFFERSONIAN believes in the primacy of science. Although Jefferson (reluctantly and somewhat inadvertently) helped to create our political party system, he found partisanship repulsive and believed that most human problems lend themselves to common sense, nonpartisan solutions. He believed that science (knowledge) is virtually infallible, that the more knowledge we accumulate the more intelligent will be our solutions to problems. He would be appalled by the politicization of science in our time—with the result that each side in a lawsuit lines up "experts" not to speak the truth but to promote a certain point of view, and that on such questions as global warming, the effect of acid rain, the usefulness of stem cell research, "scientists" are inevitably lined up on both sides. Jefferson understood, of course, that not all scientists will agree on all subjects, but he believed their core commitment to objectivity and truth would produce substantial consensus on most issues. Jefferson would be disposed to defer to the dictates of science on virtually every issue.

The gigantic advances of science between 1826 and 2003 would have thrilled Jefferson. Except for quantum indeterminacy, the progress of science has vindicated Jefferson's view that there is almost nothing that is not knowable. Today he would be disposed to believe even more completely that man is essentially (as Baron d'Holbach argued) a very ingenious kind of machine, the workings of which we will come to understand with greater and greater clarity in the course of time, until illness (including the kind of mental instability that bedeviled his son-in-law Thomas

Mann Randolph and his protégé Meriwether Lewis) would be made to disappear altogether. Jefferson was a profound materialist who believed that the soul is corpuscular, and that there was no independent soul or spirit beyond the material workings of the body. This is more than many of the best scientists believe today, but Jefferson's conviction that most of the so-called mysteries of life, including moods and the workings of the brain, are capable of being understood scientifically, has largely been vindicated, and it is quite likely that we are still in the incunabula of research on the chemistry of life.

Jefferson would be thrilled by today's space program, oceanic research, modern cartographical methods, the mapping of the genetic code, modern medicine, biochemistry, nanotechnology, crop hybridization and genetic manipulation, the possibilities of cloning, the engineering (and materials) of bridges, buildings, tunnels, and highways, irrigation systems, tracking systems, and much more.

And he would know that in essential respects we are still living in the adolescence of the engineering revolution.

Jeffersonians are not afraid of science and technology. They are steadfastly aware of the limitations of science, and they do whatever it takes to stay close to nature in a world increasingly fabricated by inert materials, but they realize that the careful use of science and technology is infinitely preferable to any form of nostalgia or Luddism.

With respect to what are termed polite manners, without sacrificing too much the sincerity of language, I would wish my countrymen to adopt just so much of European politeness, as to be ready to make all those little sacrifices of self, which really render European manners amiable, and relieve society from the disagreeable scenes to which rudeness often subjects it. Here, it seems that a man might pass a life without encountering a single rudeness. In the pleasures of the table, they are far before us, because, with good taste they unite temperance. They do not terminate the most sociable meals by transforming themselves into brutes. I have never yet seen a man drunk in France, even among the lowest of the people.

Jefferson to Charles Bellini
September 30, 1785

Renaissance Man

A **JEFFERSONIAN** tries to be a Renaissance Man (or Woman). Like his hero Francis Bacon, Jefferson took all knowledge (except geology) to be his province. Jefferson was a gifted amateur who could survey a field, determine latitude and longitude, draw a map, tie an artery, write learnedly on the development of English prosody, conduct a systematic archaeological dig, press and classify plants, dance the minuet, play the violin, and classify a library.

Jefferson is the patron saint of generalists, of gifted dilettantes, of deep dabblers, of those who eschew a narrowly focused expertise in work or in the art of living. Jefferson believed that life is nearly equally interesting on all fronts. Concentration and specialization were anathema to Thomas Jefferson. Jeffersonians are willing to try new things, and they are constantly re-inventing themselves, without losing sight of their core values and ideals. A Jeffersonian reads all the review journals as a kind of menu of which books to purchase or borrow in the next months, and tries to stay abreast with what is happening in the world on a range of fronts. A Jeffersonian finds her or his ignorance intolerable, and strives always to learn as much as can be learned given the pace and the constraints of industrial life in the twenty-first century.

Like all Renaissance individuals, a Jeffersonian is as interested in action as in ideas. There is nothing aloof or merely bookish about a Jeffersonian. Jefferson took exercise every day of his life, and he was constantly tinkering, putting his hands in the soil, working with tools, manipulating the plastics of his universe to see what benefits he might draw from them. The

Jeffersonian camps one weekend and attends a conference the next, writes letters by day and dances at night, hikes, walks, runs, explores, reads, swims, cooks, designs, decorates, travels, sews, weaves, draws, paints, builds, grows, trims, trains, communicates, and, of course, reads incessantly.

Like Jefferson, the Jeffersonian grows in energy and inspiration from all of this dizzying activity. And, like Jefferson, constantly invents new ways to increase the range and diversity of the good life.

At a time when most individuals are winding down and beginning to wait for death, Jefferson invented the University of Virginia, the darling project of his last decade. Though harmony and repose were amongst his most cherished values, Jefferson could not resist the urge to do one more great thing with his life's energy, to create a temple in which the Enlightenment and the ideals of the American republic could find continued, indeed permanent, expression.

The Jeffersonian, like I.F. Stone, takes up ancient Greek late in life for the sheer pleasure of reading the dialogues of Plato. Jeffersonians maintain the fires of creativity and curiosity right up to the last days of their lives.

If once the people become inattentive to the public affairs, you and I, Congress and Assemblies, Judges and Governors, shall all become wolves. It seems to be the law of our general nature, in spite of individual exceptions; and experience declares that man is the only animal which devours his own kind.

Jefferson to Edward Carrington
1787

Citizenship

A **JEFFERSONIAN** believes that citizenship requires much more than occasional voting. Jefferson envisioned active rather than apathetic citizens, and he would be appalled by our propensity to define an American as a consumer rather than a civic individual. Jefferson would surely argue that the American people have no just cause to grumble when they freely abdicate so much of their sovereignty to politicians who pay so little real attention to their interests. Given our infrastructure of citizenship (C-SPAN, the World Wide Web, the Internet, public broadcasting), Jefferson would argue that there has never been a time in world history when the average citizen was in a better position to participate in self-government and influence the course of events at so little cost.

A Jeffersonian has no choice but to take part in civic life, no matter how time-consuming, frustrating, or enervating it becomes. The Jeffersonian is the sole voice of reason on the local school board. Jefferson was firmly convinced that we could remain a republic only if we exhibit eternal vigilance, and force the commonwealth's formal structures to exhibit unending respect for the dignities and the will of the people. To behave passively toward government is to abdicate the idea of self-government and to give tacit approval to the independent validity of government. Jefferson intended government to be a genuine expression of the will of the people, not a permanent institution that has its own dynamics, which can exist apart from a continual supply of support from the people. In a sense, Jefferson's government is an entity that can be kept aloft only if the people (not everyone all of the time, but each one some of the time) raise their arms to support it. The minute a substantial percentage of the population turns away to private pursuits, the government falls, because it no longer rests upon the actual strength of the people.

For Jefferson, self-government really means self-government, not some tepid brand of citizenship that involves national service only if conscripted, taxation (all by way of silent withholdings), voting every fourth, or possibly second year, and purely verbal protest on those few occasions when one's ox has apparently been gored. The passivity of this would not offend Jefferson, but it would require him to conclude that such minimalist participation in the democratic process does not constitute citizenship, and that it precludes the idea of a republic.

Jefferson actually believed that over the course of time we would come to govern ourselves directly, that is, that each individual would internalize the ideals of the commonwealth and become a fully self-restraining human being, and that what formal government there was would be extremely small and modest in its scope. In the meantime, each citizen would be a jealous protector of her or his liberty, would bristle at any evidence of governmental self-aggrandizement, and would be prepared to withdraw support from government any time it exhibited a pattern of neglect, abuse, or unauthorized growth.

Jeffersonians believe that protest is one of the most important tools of citizenship and that a republic embraces rather than dismisses its discontented individuals.

Family Farming

I think our governments will remain virtuous for many centuries; as long as [the people] are chiefly agricultural, and this will be as long as there shall be vacant lands in any part of America. When they get piled upon one another in large cities, as in Europe, they will become corrupt as in Europe.

Jefferson to James Madison
1787

Family Farming

A **JEFFERSONIAN** believes in the dignity and primacy of family agriculture. Long live North Dakota! In Jefferson's time, more than ninety percent of the American people lived on self-sufficiency farms. Because they fed themselves, clothed themselves, and sheltered themselves, these farmers exemplified the self-reliance that Jefferson believed was the essential quality of a good citizen in a republic. Jefferson believed that Nature is the great teacher of humankind, that life at its core is actually quite simple, that the macrobiotic business of life is more important than politics or opera or even great literature. So he had a very special place in his heart and his philosophy for family farmers. Jefferson's profoundest words were, "Those who labor in the earth are the chosen people of God, if ever He had a chosen people, whose breasts He has made His peculiar deposit for substantial and genuine virtue."

Today only two percent of the American people live on family farms, and most of them are Hamiltonian agri-producers rather than the sort of subsistence-plus farmers that Jefferson had in mind. Most Jeffersonians do not live on farms nowadays, but they honor family farmers as a kind of irreplaceable rump of specially important citizens who can remind us of things that the rest of us tend to forget or ignore. They also see family farmers as the historically most important exemplars of the dignity of honest labor and of the nation that Jefferson intended and would still probably advocate in spite of the social, technological, and economic revolutions that have occurred since Jefferson's time.

The people are the only censors of their governors: and even their errors will tend to keep these to the true principles of their institution. To punish these errors too severely would be to suppress the only safeguard of the public liberty. The way to prevent these irregular interpositions of the people is to give them full information of their affairs thro' the channel of the public papers, and to contrive that those papers should penetrate the whole mass of the people. The basis of our governments being the opinion of the people, the very first object should be to keep that right; and were it left to me to decide whether we should have a government without newspapers, or newspapers without a government I should not hesitate a moment to prefer the latter.

Jefferson to Edward Carrington
January 16, 1787

World Citizen

A JEFFERSONIAN is a cosmopolitan. A Jeffersonian feels at home anywhere on earth, travels when she or he can, studies the history and literature of other cultures, and takes pride in maintaining a global rather than a merely national perspective. Without ever ceasing to be a good American, a Jeffersonian feels appreciation for the customs and habits of other peoples, and avoids merely carrying his or her own culture across national boundaries. Jeffersonians believe in immersion in other civilizations and they apprehend those cultures with curiosity and wonder rather than judgment. Jeffersonians regard foreign cultures as mirrors through which they are privileged to look at themselves with a new commitment to reason and a new understanding of the artificiality of their own habits and systems. Jeffersonians study foreign languages, not for the Hamiltonian purpose of increasing competitive advantage in commerce, but to attempt to see the world through the eyes of people who live by different ways and means. Jeffersonians learn Spanish to be able to read Cervantes' *Don Quixote* in the original. They study Latin not to increase their vocabularies, but to have the pleasure of reading Horace and Vergil in their marvelous native cadences. They learn ancient Greek not to gain authority for their Biblical interpretations, but to deepen their love affair with Homer and Plutarch.

The Delights of Correspondence

If it is possible to be certainly conscious of anything, I am conscious of feeling no difference between writing to the highest or lowest being on earth.

Jefferson to James Monroe, 1801

I do not know how far you may suffer, as I do, under the persecution of letters, of which every mail brings a fresh load. They are letters of inquiry, for the most part, always of good will, sometimes from friends whom I esteem, but much oftener from persons whose names are unknown to me, but written kindly and civilly, and to which, therefore, civility requires answers. Perhaps the better known failure of your hand in its function of writing, may shield you in greater degree from this distress, and so far qualify the misfortune of its disability. I happened to turn to my letter-list some time ago, and a curiosity was excited to count those received in a single year. It was the year before the last. I found the number to be one thousand two hundred and sixty-seven, in any of them requiring answers of elaborate research, and all to be answered with due attention and consideration. Take an average of this number for a week or a day, and I will repeat the question suggested by other considerations in mine of the 1st. Is this life? At best it is but the life of a mill-horse, who sees no end to his circle but in death. To such a life, that of a cabbage is paradise.

Jefferson to John Adams, June 27, 1822

The Delights of Correspondence

A JEFFERSONIAN is a writer of letters. Jefferson's basic form of communication, and his basic method of making sense of life, was the friendly letter. He wrote at least 22,000 of them with quill (eventually steel-nibbed) pens and expensive paper. Indeed, it may fairly be said that Jefferson was happiest when he was alone in a room with the English language, a book, and a blank sheet of paper before him. In our late or post-literate age, it is tempting to prize other, more immediate, forms of communication. But the fact remains that there is nothing to compare with sending or receiving a letter.

Jefferson knew that staying in touch was an essential ingredient of power. His letters were designed to keep the lines of communication—and trust, friendship, respect, and obligation—open. He knew that the greatest engine of misunderstanding and disputatiousness was a lapse into silence. He kept up his end, and he constantly rebuked his correspondents, particularly family members, for failing to write him as often and as fully as he desired.

Jeffersonians are intelligent enough not to turn their backs on cell phones, fax machines, and e-mail. But they know that there is no greater gesture of true regard, or satisfaction for that matter, than the sending and receiving of handwritten letters.

Life in Nature

There is not a sprig of grass that shoots uninteresting to me.

Jefferson to Martha Jefferson Randolph, 1790

Life in Nature

A JEFFERSONIAN is a lover of nature. Jefferson walked almost every day. Or rode a horse. Or worked in his fields or his gardens. In Jefferson's day more than ninety percent of all Americans lived on farms. Most Americans were, therefore, infinitely closer to nature than we are in the twenty-first century. Jefferson believed that life close to nature made humans saner, wiser, happier, and more virtuous than life at any remove from the earth. That's why he called farmers "the chosen people of God." But he also purchased the Natural Bridge in western Virginia because he wanted to protect from adverse development what he considered one of the sublimest places in America. In a sense Jefferson was the father of the national park system, because he believed that America exhibited Nature in her finest and least disturbed form and that it was in our national interest to preserve the sublime for the refreshment of the human spirit.

Jefferson believed that Nature redeems, restores, and reclaims humanity, and that nature is where we observe natural law in its most organic form. In other words, nature is not for Jefferson just a Wordsworthian arena for meditation and renewal, but also the best possible teacher of what is good and valuable in the world. We put our hands in the soil to make contact with the surest guide to life, and the supreme teacher of humility and good sense. We go to nature to discern the Newtonian laws of everything.

Most Jeffersonians would like to live on farms, but don't. They do tend to grow a few things, however, no matter how confined or urban their living space. It is not the quantity that counts, but the commitment to let nature's fecundity and nature's cycles influence the rhythms of our lives that makes us Jeffersonians. Today, Jeffersonians are as apt to listen to nature in their walks; on sojourns in the national parks, forests, wildlife refuges, and wilderness; camping; riding horses; kayaking rivers; mountain climbing; as in growing food. The important thing is that Jeffersonians can never stay away from nature in one of its primary forms for very long.

Jeffersonians agree with the master's commitment to stewardship. Jefferson introduced a seven-year crop rotation system to his farms to protect them from the havoc of corn and tobacco monoculture. Along with his son-in-law Thomas Mann Randolph, he introduced contour plowing in Albemarle County. He planted shelter belts. He criticized his fellow Virginians for preferring to open new fields rather than to bring true husbandry to what they already had. "The earth belongs in usufruct to the living,"[17] Jefferson wrote to James Madison, by which he meant that we have natural rights to the fruits of the earth, but we do not have the right to impair the fruitfulness of the earth. In other words, Jeffersonians are inevitably not just lovers of nature, but conservationists. Jeffersonians necessarily practice a moderate variety of environmentalism, because they agree with the Sage of Monticello that natural resources exist to serve the needs of humankind, and that government is not the best judge of which resources shall be exploited and which left alone.

The important thing is that nature matters to Jeffersonians and they get themselves into the open air as often and as purely as possible. They are friends to nature, they argue from nature, and they do what they can to make sure that nature continues to be available for the benefit of all Americans.

17. To Madison, September 6, 1789.

Summary

I know you are too honest a patriot not to wish to see our country prosper by any means, though they be not exactly those you would have preferred; and that you are too well informed a politician, too good a judge of men, not to know, that the ground of liberty is to be gained by inches, that we must be contented to secure what we can get, from time to time, and eternally press forward for what is yet to get. It takes time to persuade men to do even what is for their own good.

Jefferson to Charles Clay
January 27, 1790

Summary

THESE ARE the main outlines of a Jeffersonian outlook. The strengths of Jefferson's vision are obvious. We would live in an immeasurably better world if Jefferson's views were more widely applied to the problems of life, of individual success, of statecraft, and of citizenship. Given the choice between Jefferson's universe, or any existing alternative, no rational being would resist the reign of a second American Enlightenment.

But the weaknesses of Jefferson's vision are equally obvious at the beginning of the twenty-first century. Jefferson misunderstood the place of the irrational in human affairs. He saw the irrational as un-reason and primitiveness, but he could not see it as mystery, spirituality, or soulfulness. The fundamental problem of the materialist-secularist-rational model of life is that it has not discovered a way to devise a restraining mechanism on human manipulation of the world around it that squares with any acceptable idea of individualism and freedom of action. In other words, if government won't restrain the excesses at the heart of the human condition, and education has been starved nearly to death by the state and by the people themselves, and the realms of the spirit are ignored or disbelieved, what keeps us from spinning dangerously out of control as restless individuals and corporations? This is the critique that all fundamentalists, especially Islamists, raise against the United States at the beginning of the twenty-first century.

The Jeffersonian worldview has much more successfully advocated radical individualism than the equally important commonwealth energies of the

American people. It seems likely that the next phase of enlightened civilization is going to require a much greater integration of rational and irrational energies in the individual and in societies. By believing or pretending that the irrational was not fundamental to human experience, Jefferson effectively abandoned it to its own libidinal energies, when he ought to have attempted to channel and discipline it, in the manner of Carl Jung. It seems clear to many that we are now a runaway materialist empire and that the most important work of the soul has been neglected in western civilization, and particularly in American civilization.

The next great advance in the human project will come from a re-integration of the soul and body and spirit and mind and material world, and in some ways the hyper-rationalist Thomas Jefferson is the last person who could be depended on to lead us beyond those boundaries into the Louisiana Purchase of the soul.

Furthermore, the Jeffersonian lifestyle (although not perhaps the worldview) is unmistakably classist. Jefferson believed (naively) that virtually everyone could be a "little Jefferson," and live in Palladian orderliness, surrounded by the finer things in life. We know better. As the twenty-first century begins, Jeffersonians must learn how to incorporate the grace and beauty of the master into their daily lives without unduly separating themselves from the mass of humanity. Failure to face this challenge will both marginalize them and betray Jefferson's fundamental commitment to enlightenment for all the people, not merely "a favored few, booted and spurred, ready to ride them legitimately by the grace of God."[18] Jeffersonians must be elegant egalitarians or they will cease to win or deserve the respect of those around them.

18. To Roger Weightman, June 24, 1826.

It seems abundantly clear that we need a new Jeffersonian party in the United States, one that is based on the ideals of the founder, but which attempts to preserve the best of those ideals with good sense and flexibility, and doesn't miscarry on the rock of literalism. Jefferson has been dead for two hundred years, and some parts of his vision and his outlook are no longer useful to us. We need to clarify and preserve and diffuse those parts of his core vision that are still vital to the success of the American experiment and which have been eroded severely as the United States has moved to its new status as economic and at times military world empire.

It is not necessary to embody every one of these principles to be a good Jeffersonian. Jefferson was convinced that no one style was appropriate for all people. The essence of freedom is located in our empowerment to pursue happiness in our own way. Although Jefferson took pleasure in prescribing behavior to his protégés and insisting that discipline and system were essential ingredients of the successful life, we are free to discriminate between those Jeffersonian ideas that resonate with our twenty-first century souls and those that do not. Generally speaking, however, the more of these habits and principles one masters, the more Jeffersonian one becomes. They represent an integrated view of life, and people with a Jeffersonian bent usually find little to quibble with in his strictures.

Thomas Jefferson is not the panacea. But his ideals and his vision are the lens through which we must again explore American possibilities if we wish to be an enlightenment people and not merely a rich, powerful, haughty nation state. Above all, we must attempt to renew our constitutional culture so that we can, without blushing, call ourselves a republic again.

What Does All this Mean in Practical Terms?

Of all exercises walking is best. . . . No one knows, till he tries, how easily a habit of walking is acquired. A person who never walked three miles will in the course of a month become able to walk 15 or 20 without fatigue. I have known some great walkers & had particular accounts of many more; and I never knew or heard of one who was not healthy & long lived. This species of exercise therefore is much to be advised.

Jefferson to Thomas Mann Randolph, Jr.,
August 27, 1786

What Does All this Mean in Practical Terms?

TURN OFF your television. In fact, give it away. Walk every day, the farther the better, preferably in the natural rather than the civilized world. Learn at least one other politically or culturally significant language. Start now, no matter how old you are. Take up a musical instrument and get good enough at it to entertain your friends. At any rate, try to bring mastery to all that you do, or at least to some central expressions of your soul. Get and stay healthy. Avoid excesses of food and drink. Write long, lucid letters to your friends and family. Take an active role in your civic life. Love your family more than the world. Take up a craft. Experiment boldly, and don't be afraid to re-invent your life. Behave as if there is nothing your government can or should do for you. Regard self-reliance and resourcefulness as the defining principles of your life. Host splendid dinner parties, where the emphasis is on gracious and intelligent conservation rather than on ostentation. Build your dream house, or at least rework the one you have until it becomes an unmistakable expression of your value system and your view of the world. Grow something and ingest it with pride. Defend liberty—your own and others'—even if it makes you unpopular. Get the facts. Argue without passion or rancor. Be a champion of education. Tolerate difference. Seek harmony in all that you do. Ask perennially: Is it reasonable? Is it healthy? Is it useful? Can it be improved? Never waste a single moment. Drive your children to excellence.

Above all, surround yourself with good books, and grant yourself plenty of time to read them. Sit serenely, bathed in natural illumination, with the best glass of wine you can afford, and read for hours at a stretch, with the confidence that in doing so you are fulfilling the highest purposes of humankind.

Aspire to live according to the dictates of reason. Pursue happiness, but define it with good sense and dignity.

Clay S. Jenkinson

Benjamin Franklin's Approach

For those who find the idea of becoming Jeffersonians daunting, I suggest that you adopt Benjamin Franklin's practical approach. As a young man Franklin set out to achieve "moral perfection." He made a grid of the thirteen virtues he wished to acquire, and then devoted a week attempting to incorporate each virtue into his character. Thus he worked his way through the full thirteen virtues four times per year. He continued to practice this self-catechizing program in a formal manner for two years, and thereafter worked on the same cluster of virtues in a more informal way. The virtues he attempted to incorporate were:

1. **Temperance:** Eat not to dullness; drink not to elevation.

2. **Silence:** Speak not but what may benefit others or yourself; avoid trifling conversation.

3. **Order:** Let all your things have their places; let each part of your business have its time.

4. **Resolution:** Resolve to perform what you ought; perform without fail what you resolve.

5. **Frugality:** Make no expense but to do good to others or yourself; i.e., waste nothing.

6. **Industry:** Lose no time; be always employ'd in something useful; cut off all unnecessary actions.

7. **Sincerity:** Use no hurtful deceit; think innocently and justly, and, if you speak, speak accordingly.

8. **Justice:** Wrong none by doing injuries, or omitting the benefits that are your duty.

9. **Moderation:** Avoid extreams; forbear resenting injuries so much as you think they deserve.

10. **Cleanliness:** Tolerate no uncleanliness in body, cloaths, or habitation.

11. **Tranquillity:** Be not disturbed at trifles, or at accidents common or unavoidable.

12. **Chastity:** Rarely use venery but for health or offspring, never to dulness, weakness, or the injury of your own or another's peace or reputation.

13. **Humility:** Imitate Jesus and Socrates.

Franklin's virtues are somewhat different from what I believe are the essentials of the Jeffersonian lifestyle, but Jefferson would surely have approved of the idea of creating a grid and a regular course of discipline to bring about the good and integrated life. You might wish to make your own grid of Jeffersonian qualities, and work on one each week, using Franklin's method.

Thomas Jefferson's Decalogue

JEFFERSON LISTED his personal ten commandments, or what he called "A Decalogue of Canons" for observation in practical life, in a letter to a boy who had been named after him, Thomas Jefferson Smith, on February 21, 1825:

1. Never put off till to-morrow what you can do to-day.

2. Never trouble another for what you can do yourself.

3. Never spend your money before you have it.

4. Never buy what you do not want, because it is cheap; it will be dear to you.

5. Pride costs us more than hunger, thirst, and cold.

6. We never repent of having eaten too little.

7. Nothing is troublesome that we do willingly.

8. How much pain have cost us the evils which have never happened.

9. Take things always by their smooth handle.

10. When angry, count ten, before you speak; if very angry, an hundred.

The best biographies of Jefferson are:

Merrill Peterson, *Thomas Jefferson and the New Nation.*

Alf J. Mapp, *Thomas Jefferson: A Strange Case of Mistaken Identity.*

Dumas Malone, *Thomas Jefferson and His Times* (six volumes).

Noble Cunningham, *In Pursuit of Reason: The Life of Thomas Jefferson.*

For books about how Jefferson might see our world, see:

Garret Ward Sheldon, *What Would Jefferson Say? What Our Third President Would Think of the World Today—from the Budget Deficit and Race Relations to Freedom of Speech and Family Values.*

Thomas G. West, *Vindicating the Founders: Race, Sex, Class, and Justice in the Origins of America.*

Coy Barefoot, *Thomas Jefferson and Leadership: Executive Lessons from His Life and Letters.*

Harrold Hellenbrand, *The Unfinished Revolution: Education and Politics in the Thought of Thomas Jeferson.*

Walter Russell Mead, *Special Providence: American Foreign Policy and How It Changed the World.*

Ten great books about Jefferson:

Silvio A. Bedini, *Thomas Jefferson: Statesman of Science.*

Joseph Ellis, *American Sphinx: The Character of Thomas Jefferson.*

Daniel Boorstin, *The Lost World of Thomas Jefferson.*

Jack McLaughlin, *Jefferson and Monticello: The Biography of a Builder.*

Karl Lehmann, *Thomas Jefferson: American Humanist.*

Annette Gordon-Reed, *Thomas Jefferson and Sally Hemings: An American Controversy.*

Albert J. Nock, *Jefferson.*

Garry Wills, *Inventing America: Jefferson's Declaration of Independence.*

Leonard Levy, *Jefferson and Civil Liberties: The Darker Side.*

Forrest McDonald, *The Presidency of Thomas Jefferson.*

Glossary

ACLU. The American Civil Liberties Union was founded in New York in 1920. The ACLU exists to champion and protect civil liberties in the United States. Annoying though the ACLU is to social conservatives, it is hard to imagine a more Jeffersonian institution in the United States. It advocates a strict observance of civil liberties, especially at times when erosion of such liberties would be supported by a majority of the population.

American Philosophical Society. Created in 1743 (the year of Jefferson's birth) by Benjamin Franklin, the American Philosophical Society was the most prestigious national intellectual organization in the United States. Dedicated to the pursuit of "useful knowledge," the society was more committed to science than to philosophy per se. Thomas Jefferson was the third president of the APS. He was first elected to membership on January 21, 1780.

Arcadia, Horatian. The Roman poet Horace (65-8 BCE) envisioned a sweet pastoral world of thoughtful and self-sufficient family farmers who lived away from the centers of power and sought happiness and fecundity rather than power, money, and glory. Horace was a satirist of the genial school. Arcadia was an ancient region of Greece, in the Peloponnese, that came to represent a pastoral paradise in the Greek and Roman imagination.

Bacon, Francis. 1561-1626. According to Jefferson, another of the three greatest men who ever lived. Philosopher, lawyer, statesman, man of letters, courtier, and promoter of the scientific method. Bacon is now best known for his famous *Essays*, but Jefferson admired him chiefly for his *Advancement of Learning* (1605) and the *Novum Organum* (1620), both of which argued for a reorganization of knowledge and the clearing away of medieval habits of thought. Bacon famously took all knowledge to be his province.

Cervantes. 1547-1616. The great Spanish novelist, whose *Don Quixote* first appeared in 1605. The story of the romantic superannuated knight Don Quixote, his fat traveling companion Sancho Panza and his decrepit horse Rosinante captured the world's imagination, including that of Jefferson, who said that Don Quixote was one of the only novels he ever read more than once.

Cicero, Marcus Tullius. 106-43 BCE. Roman writer, lawyer, philosopher, statesman, and ardent republican. Almost forgotten today, Cicero was, in Jefferson's time, the most important figure from the classical world. Fifty-eight orations and 900 of Cicero's letters are extant. Jefferson admired Cicero as a republican advocate, but disliked his ornate and complex prose style.

Condorcet. 1743-1794. French mathematician, statesman, and man of letters. He is sometimes called the "last of the philosophes." In spite of a difficult life, which ended in a French revolutionary prison, Condorcet embodied the optimism of the Enlightenment. He believed in the perfectibility of humankind. Jefferson admired him deeply.

Cosway, Maria. 1759-1838. Italian-British painter, with whom Jefferson fell head-over-heels in love in 1786. Unfortunately she was already married to the painter Richard Cosway, who was one of the finest miniaturists of the eighteenth century. On October 12, 1786, Jefferson wrote Mrs. Cosway an eleven-page love letter, now usually referred to as "My Head and My Heart."

Diderot, Denis. 1713-1784. Jefferson just missed the chance to meet the chief editor of the famous *French Encyclopedie*, which was one of the principal works of the Enlightenment. Diderot was one of the busiest and most productive of the philosophes, the reformers, journalists, and men of letters of French Enlightenment society. Diderot is also considered the first great art critic. He believed that all received ideas needed to be examined according to the dictates of reason and good sense.

The Enlightenment. The optimistic, rational, and reformist Euro-American intellectual movement of the seventeenth and eighteenth centuries. Represented by such European thinkers as Voltaire, Rousseau, Locke, Samuel Johnson, Diderot, Condorcet, D'Holbach, and Montesquieu. The two principal American exemplars of the Enlightenment were Benjamin Franklin and Thomas Jefferson. The Enlightenment was characterized by reason, skepticism, contempt for received tradition, optimism, and a belief in the essential goodness of humankind. The Enlightenment tended to prefer Deism to a faith and miracle-based Christianity. The Enlightenment believed that reason and good sense could together reform most of the existing institutions of the world.

Epicurean. The Greek philosopher Epicurus (341-270 BCE) believed the gods are beautiful and serene beings entirely removed from the day-to-day governance of the world. In ethics, Epicurus identified the purpose of life as the rational pursuit of pleasure. Happiness is virtuous pleasure and the absence of pain. Jefferson regarded himself as an Epicurean, but he rebuked his protégé William Short for seeking self-indulgent rather than disciplined pleasure.

Federalists. The political party of Hamilton, Washington, John Adams, Fisher Ames, Rufus King, and John Jay. After helping to create the U.S. Constitution in 1787, and promote it through the Federalist Papers and in state ratification struggles, the Federalists helped to set up the actual apparatus of the national government during the first twelve years of the republic. After Jefferson came to power in 1800, in what he called the Second American Revolution, the Federalists quickly faded from power. Hamilton's death in July 1804 left Federalism without a brilliant national leader.

Franklin, Benjamin. 1706-1790. The most important thing to remember is that Franklin was a full generation older than most of the Founding Fathers. Jefferson revered him as the perfect exemplar of what America represents: born common and poor, self-made, a natural aristocrat of the highest achievement. Inventor, scientist, newspaperman, diplomat, man of letters, raconteur, humorist, political theorist. Invented many American institutions, including the public library, unicameral legislatures, and the volunteer fire department. Jefferson idolized him, in part because Franklin was so adroit as America's first representative in Europe.

Hamilton, Alexander. 1755?-1804. The brilliant, focused policy wonk who was the first and perhaps greatest Secretary of the Treasury. Born in obscurity in the Caribbean, Hamilton rose by the sheer force of his genius to be one of the most important men in American history. He stood for strong central government, a large peacetime military establishment, a mixed economy, the national debt, and a forward and engaged foreign policy.

Author of the majority of the outstanding Federalist Papers. He despised the people. Hamilton was killed in a duel by Aaron Burr on July 11, 1804.

Homer. Ninth or eighth century BCE. The author of the *Iliad* and the *Odyssey*, which Jefferson regarded as the two most delightful books ever written. Jefferson read Homer in the original Greek.

Jung, Carl. 1875-1961. Swiss psychiatrist. Best known for *The Psychology of the Unconscious* (1912), and *Memories, Dreams, Reflections* (1962). Jung argued that the integrated individual turned towards, not away from, the dark energies in the soul, and came to terms with them rather than regarded the shadow as alien.

Locke, John. 1632-1704. According to Jefferson, one of the three greatest men who ever lived. Philosopher and political theorist. Although he is now best remembered for his *Second Treatise on Government* (1690), he was best known in Jefferson's time for his "Essay Concerning Human Understanding" (1690), which argued that the mind at birth is a blank slate (tabula rasa), on which one's personality and sensibilities are eventually inscribed by reason and experience.

Ludditism. Opposition to industrial machinery that displaces workers. The Luddites or Ludds were named for a (probably fictitious) leader Ned Ludd. The movement began in 1811 in Nottingham, England. Luddites opposed the mechanization of labor and sometimes destroyed textile machinery that they regarded as a threat to their craft.

Madison, James. 1751-1836. Jefferson's closest friend, perhaps the greatest of the Founding Fathers. Jefferson called him "the greatest farmer in the world." Madison was the principal architect of the U.S. Constitution of

1787, the author of the Bill of Rights, and the Fourth President of the United States. He was Jefferson's pragmatic censor, apologist, and protector. Jefferson lifted Madison to higher idealism. Madison held Jefferson down to earth (at least closer). Jefferson's last words to Madison were, "take care of me when dead." Madison, dutiful and loyal as always, did just that.

Newton, Isaac. 1642-1727. The third of Jefferson's three greatest men who ever lived. Mathematician, genius, physicist, the inventor of calculus, and the originator of the theory of universal gravitation. Newton was chiefly interesting to the Enlightenment because he symbolized the uses of reason and science, and proved that beneath the seeming complexity of the universe men of discernment could find simple and universal underlying laws.

Novus ordo seclorum. New order of the ages. The motto appears on the reverse of the Great Seal of the United States. It also appears on the back of the U.S. dollar bill. It is originally a motto of the Freemasonry movement.

Palladian. Characterized by order, symmetry, and neoclassicism. The Italian architect Andrea Palladio (1508-1580) attempted to recreate (and update) the Roman villa as the basis of his many building designs. He employed the ancient Greek and Roman temple front for the porticos he designed. His *Four Treatises on Architecture* has proved to be one of the most influential books ever written about design. Jefferson owned four copies of the *Treatises*, which he regarded as the bible of his own design efforts. Monticello, Poplar Forest (Jefferson's second home), and the University of Virginia were all Palladian.

Plutarch. 46?-119? CE. Greek biographer and author. All of the Founding Fathers read Plutarch's *Lives of the Noble Grecians and Romanes* (as translator Thomas North put it in 1579), the greatest compendium of leadership biographies of the ancient world. The Founders in large part shaped their own leadership styles from the pages of Plutarch. Jefferson was particularly fond of the lives of Pericles, Solon, and Cincinnatus.

Reign of Terror. 1793-94. The most violent period of the French Revolution, during which thousands of French individuals were executed without trial or legal representation. The terror was established by the French government on September 5, 1793. A law passed in June 1794 suspended the accused's right to legal defense and a fair trial. The terror ended with the overthrow of Robespierre on July 27, 1794. Jefferson lamented the excesses of the terror, but defended it as a natural effusion of the pent up frustrations of the French people.

Rousseau. 1712-1778. The most famous and the most notorious of the Enlightenment's great figures. Author of the *Social Contract*, the *Discourse on the Origin and Foundations of Inequality Among Men*, the autobiographical *Confessions*, and the greatly influential educational novel *Emile*, Rousseau was a man of letters whom Jefferson found hard to admire. He did, however, share in some part Rousseau's view that the people are always right.

Shays' Rebellion. Agrarian uprising in western Massachusetts 1786-87. Led by Revolutionary War veteran Daniel Shays, the rebels marched on the supreme court in Springfield, Massachusetts, on the nearby federal arsenal, and organized to prevent a number of foreclosures on Massachusetts farms. Reaction to the rebellion was paranoid. Jefferson was one of the few national leaders who refused to condemn the rebellion, which he considered a sign of the health of the American republic. "I like a little rebellion now and then," he said. Shays' rebellion helped to precipitate the Constitutional Convention in Philadelphia in 1787.

Small, William. 1734-1775 [?]. Jefferson's principal mentor. In 1758 at the age of 23, Small was appointed professor of natural philosophy (science) at the College of William and Mary in Virginia. Later he was a member of the International Lunar Society in Britain. Jefferson called him "a man profound in most of the useful branches of science, with a happy talent of communication, correct and gentlemanly manners, and a large and liberal mind... from his conversation I got my first views of the expansion of science and of the system of things in which we are placed."

Smith, Adam. 1723-1790. Scottish political economist and social philosopher. Smith is best known for his enormously influential *Inquiry into the Nature and Causes of the Wealth of Nations* (1776), but the book that had the greatest impact on the age of Jefferson was Smith's *Theory of Moral Sentiments* (1759). Reacting to the prevailing mercantilism of his time, Smith argued that the economy works best when based on individual self-interest. When each individual does what is best for himself in the economic arena, the whole economy seems to be guided by an "invisible hand."

Stoic. The Stoic philosophers advocated self-control, reason, and imperviousness to acute emotions, good or bad. Stoicism was founded by Zeno of Citium (in Greece) around 300 BCE. The name comes from the stoa or portico in Athens, where Zeno and the early stoics conducted their teaching. Among the stoics were

Seneca, Epictetus, and the Roman emperor Marcus Aurelius. Stoicism emphasized fate, the underlying order of the universe, and personal tranquility. Jefferson regarded himself as a modified stoic.

Stone, I.F. 1907-1989. American journalist and leftist. Stone famously decided to learn classical Greek late in life in order to read the Socratic dialogues of Plato and write a book about The Trial of Socrates.

Tabula rasa. A blank slate. The idea (ultimately Lockean) was that the mind was a blank slate at birth, and that in the course of life stimuli were inscribed on that slate. The concept was used metaphorically in other arenas. In Jefferson's mind, the continent was in some sense a tabula rasa, waiting to be inscribed by an American utopia.

De Tocqueville, Alexis. 1805-1859. French traveler, political theorist, and historian. Tocqueville visited the United States in 1832 to examine the new democratic era in world history in its purest form. His book, *Democracy in America*, published (1835-40) after Jefferson's death, is widely considered the best book ever written about America by a foreigner.

Vergil. 70-19 BCE. Roman epic poet and advocate for simple, virtuous, hard-working rural life. Vergil's *Aeneid*, the national epic of Rome, was arguably the most influential of all ancient books. Jefferson would have read Vergil, in Latin, early and often.

Voltaire. 1694-1778. The greatest of the French philosophes. Conversationalist, wit, satirist, philosopher, champion of religious liberty, man of letters, and the principal popularizer of the achievement of Isaac Newton.

Washington, George. 1732-1799. The First President of the United States. He was a better farmer than Jefferson, a better statesman, and an infinitely better warrior. And his character was less problematic. Jefferson looked up to Washington, revered him within limits, but deprecated the general's lack of deep classical education. Washington was possessed of exemplary self-discipline. Jefferson said he had the best judgment of any man he ever knew. Like Jefferson, Washington was a reckless consumer of the finer things of life, but unlike the Sage of Monticello, he had the means to pay for what he purchased.

Wythe, George. 1726-1806. Jefferson's great legal mentor. A signer of the Declaration of Independence and a Virginia delegate to the Constitutional Convention in 1787, Wythe is considered by some the first law professor in American history. In addition to Jefferson, he helped to train John Marshall, James Monroe, and Henry Clay. In 1806 he was murdered by his grand nephew George Sweeny.

HUMANITIES SCHOLAR Clay S. Jenkinson believes that our two-party system is a hopeless mess. "We don't have a two-party system. We have the greater Hamilton party and the lesser Hamilton party, but there is no real enlightenment alternative to the way America does business at home and in the world." This bold essay attempts to form the skeleton of a new Jeffersonianism in American life. "It's no use to think of Jefferson as a slaveholder or the master of Sally Hemings, or the dispossessor of American Indians," Jenkinson says. "Those things are all true, but we must not let them prevent us from seeing the positive vision of Thomas Jefferson, which we all desperately need. This book is an attempt to articulate what a Jeffersonian worldview would be at the beginning of the twenty-first century." *Becoming Jefferson's People* may possibly lead to a new political party in the United States, but it should lead to a national conversation about who we are, what we stand for, what we value, and how we wish to behave at home and abroad.

CLAY S. JENKINSON is a scholar-in-residence at Lewis & Clark College in Portland, Oregon; a senior fellow at the Center for Digital Government in California; the artistic director of the Great Basin Chautauqua in Nevada; an award winning author of five books, including *Thomas Jefferson: Man of Light, The Character of Meriwether Lewis, A Vast and Open Plain: The Writings of the Lewis and Clark Expedition in North Dakota*, and *Message on the Wind: A Spiritual Odyssey on the Northern Plains*. He lives in Reno, Nevada, and Portland, Oregon. Jenkinson grew up on the plains of North Dakota, which he describes as "the most Jeffersonian place in America."

Please Support the Marmarth Institute

CLAY S. JENKINSON'S vision of a Jeffersonian future is primarily focused on something called the Marmarth Institute. Marmarth[1] is a tiny village in extreme southwestern North Dakota, situated in one of the most beautiful stretches of the Little Missouri River. Together with the Marmarth Historical Society, Clay intends to create a splendid but modest regional think tank and retreat center in the village of Marmarth. Four buildings are earmarked for the Marmarth Institute: the Barber Auditorium, the Milwaukee Road bunkhouse, the old Milwaukee Road railroad depot, and the historic Mystic Theater.

The Marmarth Institute will explore many Jeffersonian themes, the chief of which is the future of the family farm and rural America.

Clay Jenkinson believes important parts of the national conversation can be convened in Marmarth, and that the deliberations and results can be disseminated to a much larger audience across the region, the nation, and the globe thanks to the electronic media of our time.

The day will come, Clay believes, when the Marmarth Institute is regarded as one of the most important centers of intelligence and renewal in North America. We want the Marmarth Institute to be a place, centered at the heart of the continent, where extraordinary people gather to converse, seek renewal, explore ideas, walk the land, listen to the wind, serve as Muses to each other, reconnect with the soil and the grass, and form revolutionary friendships. We want the Marmarth Institute to grow new leaders who

1. Marmarth was named in 1908 for Margaret Martha Fitch, the granddaughter of Milwaukee Road Railroad president Albert J. Farling. It is pronounced Mar-muth.

will carry new insights into the larger community. The Marmarth Institute will not be an upstart Aspen or a northern plains version of the Land Institute at Salina, Kansas. It will be a Spartan institution, not as much concerned with luxury and pleasing the privileged as with exploring the world with integrity. Marmarth is an isolated place; those who make their way to the Marmarth Institute will be self-selecting. The improbability of it will be one of its principal strengths.

Some will come to Marmarth to talk. Others will come to walk, paint, sojourn with the Badlands, write, think, milk calves, fix fences, ride horses, dream atop buttes, or sit in the Little Missouri River. Everyone who comes will work a little in the Institute or in the community. Everyone will have large stretches of unscheduled time. The emphasis will be on the authentic. Nobody will come away without having had the opportunity to come to terms with the place.

The Marmarth Institute is a large vision and it needs a great deal of help.

The Marmarth Institute needs many things—first money, and lots of it, then creative thinkers and lucid arguers, then permanent participants who will bring to it insights and skills that will keep it fresh and open-minded. The Marmarth Institute is not a pipedream. It is in some sense already in existence, and preliminary work has already begun to stabilize and restore the four principal buildings that will become the center of our activities.

The Jeffersonian Revolution will come when we craft a new vision of America so "plain and firm as to command . . . assent," as Jefferson put it to Henry Lee in 1825. Some parts of that vision are outlined in broad strokes in this book. Others will be worked out in our seminars, retreats, symposia, debates, residencies, and meditations. When the story of American renewal is written, sometime at the end of the current century, Marmarth will be remembered as an improbable miniature Philadelphia on the northern Great Plains.

If you are interested in helping the Marmarth Institute come into being, contact Clay Jenkinson at www.th-jefferson.org or Jeffysage@aol.com, or send your charitable contribution to:

Marmarth Institute
c/o Patti Perry
Marmarth Historical Society
P.O. Box 93
Marmarth, North Dakota 58643-0093

The Marmarth Historical Society is a nonprofit, 501(c)(3) corporation. Your contributions are tax deductible to the extent allowed by the law. Please consult with your tax accountant to determine your deduction.

We'll see you in Marmarth, at the glorious oxbow at the heart of the heart of the country, where the cropland breaks down and the breaks country begins.

Clay S. Jenkinson
Custodian of the Marmarth Institute

Jeffersonian Notes

Jeffersonian Notes

Jeffersonian Notes

Jeffersonian Notes

Jeffersonian Notes

Jeffersonian Notes

Jeffersonian Resolutions

Jeffersonian Resolutions

Jeffersonian Resolutions

Jeffersonian Resolutions